junk jewelry

junk jewelry

25 extraordinary designs TO CREATE FROM ordinary objects

JANE ELDERSHAW

Illustrations by Jane Eldershaw | Photography by Steven Dunbar

POTTER
CRAFT

Published in the United States by Potter Craft,
an imprint of the Crown Publishing Group, a
division of Random House, Inc., New York.
www.clarksonpotter.com
wwww.pottercraft.com

POTTER CRAFT and colophon is a
registered trademark of Random House, Inc.

Library of Congress Cataloging-in-
Publication Data is available upon request.

ISBN: 978-0-307-40517-3
Printed in China

Design by Laura Palese
Illustrations by Jane Eldershaw

10 9 8 7 6 5 4 3 2 1

First Edition

Many, many thanks

to Melissa Bonventre, Chi Ling Moy, Rosy Ngo, Laura Palese, Christina Schoen, Courtney Conroy, Kim Tyner, and the Potter Craft team; to Janet Rosen and Sheree Bykofsky for believing in me; and to Steven Dunbar for the great photographs.

Love and appreciation to Dee Anne Dyke, the most stylish woman on the planet, who graciously made available items from her collection of "Clown Jewels" for this book; to my good friend Michelle Murch, with whom I've spent many happy hours browsing through junk; to Pauline Fingleton, great neighbor, friend, and counselor; and to George Ladas, for junk jewelry ingredients and so much else.

contents

PART ③
CREATING

PART ④
WEARING

INTRODUCTION

Junk Jewelry Should Be Taken Seriously!
(AND LIGHTHEARTEDLY)

I've always been intrigued by the psychology of costume and people who use what they wear as a means to express, and even flaunt, their individuality. Style, after all, is the visible component of personality. I see the making and wearing of junk jewelry as part of today's freer, more inventive approach to getting dressed, an approach that embraces vintage, retro, and recycled fashion. I also see tech jewelry and wearable technology—phones clipped to a bracelet, security-pass necklaces, computer-storage keyrings—as part of the trend toward greater self-expression. I predict that in the future what we adorn ourselves with will become increasingly functional, useful, and meaningful. And we will want to personalize these things by wearing them together with low-tech symbols and talismans: our own personal junk.

Is it ridiculous to elevate the projects in this book—necklaces made of plastic tags, bracelets made of buttons—to the status of jewelry? Is junk jewelry—dusty old

> *Ideas are more precious than gold and silver.*
> —URSULA ILSE-NEUMAN

detritus glued onto a fake gold pin—art? Is it even a craft? That depends a lot on how it is worn, and who's wearing it. That's why I've included a section in this book about how you might put together looks based on the adornments you create. I believe that it's the thinking and conceptualizing behind junk jewelry that make it just as much art as more traditional forms of creativity.

This book is designed as an introduction to *objets trouvés* jewelry-making for beginners. I encourage you to go further, and learn the techniques of traditional jewelry-making, such as soldering and stone-setting, so you can use them to make better-quality junk jewelry. This guide is more about acquiring a visual vocabulary and having fun cheaply.

If you naturally gravitate to thrift-store funkiness, if you like to wear distinctive outfits, and if you take serious things lightly and silly things seriously, you'll enjoy making and wearing junk jewelry.

Anyone can go into Tiffany's and walk out with something sparkly. All it takes is money. To make and wear junk jewelry takes wit and chutzpa and creativity.

PART | ①

ORIGINS

WHAT IS JUNK JEWELRY AND WHERE DID IT COME FROM?

Perhaps traditional jewelry is obsolete.

IN THE PAST, GRANDIOSE DISPLAYS OF PRECIOUS STONES AND METALS WERE MEANT TO SHOWCASE A PERSON'S WEALTH AND STATUS.

Today, it's more prestigious (and fun and useful) to connect with the world by wearing the latest portable communication device.

Wearable technology and shifting social conventions have changed everything. We still use accessories to say something about ourselves, but now the vocabulary has grown significantly.

Junk jewelry (sometimes called *objets trouvés* accessories, creative salvage, or mixed-media jewelry) is witty, surreal jewelry made from found objects. This is not to be confused with costume jewelry, which is the kind of thing that Coco Chanel made popular: exuberant glass and plastic copies of gold and precious stones.

Jewelry has always sent a message—think of what a wedding ring, a flag pin, or a diamond tiara says about you. Jewelry can say, "Look at the beauty of what I'm wearing!" Or "This represents someone dear to me!" Or "I value this object highly!" We can say the same things with junk jewelry, but junk jewelry also sends this message: I have a sense of humor. It does so by poking fun at real jewelry, by replacing diamonds and pearls with unexpected items, and in so doing, elevates these found items to the status of jewelry.

Junk jewelry is more personal, too. Using something you love as a jewel is meaningful in a way that purchasing an anonymous semiprecious stone is not. It's a more literal and truer representation of your image, in part because it has less to do with the inherent worth of the components. Gemstones and precious metals are associated with wealth; the junk you choose has lots more interesting associations.

For example, junk jewelry allows for subtle commentary on how you see yourself and your surroundings: You can make a visual pun by wearing, say, a Dalmatian pin with your black-and-white outfit. You can parody a uniform by pinning medals you've made to your blazer. You can brighten up rainy days by wearing tiny umbrella earrings. You can honor the spirit of a garden party by donning your collection of bee and dragonfly jewelry.

In this way, junk jewelry provides not only visual but intellectual enjoyment. You create a dissonance when you wear an object in an unexpected way. The observer does a double take, recognizing that something usually associated with one environment is now front and center in another, in a totally incongruous manner. It's a visual punch line—we have to make the same sort of tiny mental leap that's involved when we laugh at a cartoon or "get" a joke.

> *Using something you love as a jewel is meaningful in a way that purchasing an anonymous semi-precious stone is not.*

Those who create this edgy, eccentric jewelry observe the world differently than most of us. Like Picasso, they have the ability to look at a jumble of old bicycle parts and envision them as a sculpture in the form of a bull's head. And, in fact, junk jewelry is not often made by regular jewelers, but by artists or sculptors who work in many mediums, one of which happens to be jewelry.

The initial inspiration for junk jewelry was perhaps the found object assemblages of the Dada artists. Dada was an artistic movement that emerged around 1915, in reaction to the horrors of World War I. Marshall McLuhan has said that "Art is whatever you can get away with," and the Dadaists took this kind of thinking to extremes. Their confrontational, nihilistic influence can be seen in subsequent art trends, such as in-your-face performance art. But certain fashion designers also embraced the Dada doctrine, and examples of it have been appearing on runways for the last twenty years. These are just some of the surreal accessories designers have used recently in their collections:

In the early 1980s KARL LAGERFELD'S collections for Chloé used brooches in the shape of faucets as well as piano keyboard bracelets and belts. He designed a fauteuil brooch—a miniature armchair—that was featured in the September 1985 issue of *Vanity Fair*. The photograph showed the model sitting on an armchair wearing an armchair-shaped hat.

The late Italian designer FRANCO MOSCHINO created a handbag in the shape of an iron, and one that looked as if it were covered in melted chocolate.

CHANEL featured earrings made of tiny audio-tape cassettes in 2004.

PAUL SMITH'S accessories for 2004 included trompe l'oeil tea cups, pastries, and little glasses of red wine on handbags and key chains.

JEFFREY CHOW, for his spring 2005 New York fashion show, designed a bed jacket made of sequins hand-punched from Coca-Cola cans.

MARTIN MARGIELA sent models down the runway in fall 2005 wearing long white dresses and necklaces of colored ice cubes that slowly melted dripping colors onto their garments.

In 2006 Hermès designer JEAN PAUL GAULTIER included a leather dog collar worn as a necklace in his collection.

All pure Dada! But perhaps these modern designers have also been influenced by the jewelry of two famous couturières and the Surrealist art movement of the last century.

COCO CHANEL: jewelry BECOMES fun

. . . fake pearls, cut-glass cabochon necklaces, giant-sized earrings— piled on, gypsy-style. It's the jewelry that gives the Chanel look a faintly naughty edge, that makes it ambiguous and interesting in a way the clothes by themselves are not.
—HOLLY BRUBACH

Coco Chanel (1883–1971) almost single-handedly gave costume jewelry its contemporary cachet and supposedly coined the term *junk jewelry* (although she didn't use the words to mean found-object junk jewelry). She did this by wearing jewelry in ways that were completely new for her time. She was not ashamed of her fakes; moreover, she mixed them with the real thing—faux pearls with cultured pearls, gilt with gold, Maltese crosses with Byzantine ones. She made wearing huge amounts of jewelry look chic and elegant, even with daytime fabrics like tweed.

It is said that Chanel had the real jewelry her admirers gave her copied in colored glass—but made bigger and glitzier than the originals. Legend also has it that to avoid the cost of insurance she wore all of it at all times, and said, "It doesn't matter if they are real, as long as they look like junk!"

Sketch inspired by a photograph of Chanel earrings worn by a model in February 2004.

ELSA SCHIAPARELLI: THE DESIRE TO shock

For those who love to dress with quirky individuality, fashion designer Elsa Schiaparelli (1890–1973) is an inspiration and an icon. Born in Italy, she had a couture house in Paris from the late 1920s until 1954.

Schiaparelli loved to shock. This is the woman who created a handbag that looked like a birdcage, another that played music when it was opened, and gloves with red snakeskin "fingernails." She put together avant-garde color combinations: turquoise with grape, purple and olive green with dark red. She urged her customers not to match, handing them one mauve glove and one yellow glove to wear with a black evening gown. And, of course, her signature color was "shocking pink."

Schiaparelli was ahead of her time. She was the first to use fabric printed with newsprint (a collage of her own press clippings), the first to create Plexiglas bracelets and earrings, and the first to consider zippers to be decorative as well as functional. She created glow-in-the-dark phosphorescent pins to help the wearer find her way on the street at night. She was one of the first to advocate wearing multiple earrings on one ear, and she commissioned a design for a three-part ring—a ring that fit around each joint of a single finger, including one that covered the nail.

And Schiaparelli employed the leading Surrealist and Dada artists of the day to create accessories for her collections. She had a jacket inspired by Jean Cocteau embroidered with hands that looked as if they were clasping a waist. Her "desk" dress, inspired by the Spanish Surrealist Salvador Dali, had pockets that looked like drawers. Dali also created surreal hats for her: a shoe hat, an ice-cream cone hat, and a mutton-chop hat.

A fur-covered bracelet from one of Schiaparelli's collections is said to have inspired the artist Meret Oppenheim to create his famous teacup and saucer covered in fur.

The Dada artist Man Ray photographed a necklace Schiaparelli codesigned with poet Louis Aragon, which was made to look as if it were composed of a string of aspirin tablets. (Man Ray also photographed Mina Loy wearing a thermometer as an earring on her right ear, and Meret Oppenheim wearing champagne cork earrings.)

For the junk jewelry fan, Schiaparelli's ideas are truly inspiring: a collarlike necklace of clear plastic embedded with fake, but very realistic-looking insects—she

Schiaparelli's necklace of insects trapped in Perspex, which she created around the years of 1937–1938. The original is housed in the Brooklyn Museum, New York.

wanted the look of insects crawling over the neck. (Today, similar jewelry is being made using real bugs set in resin.) She also commissioned a charm bracelet made of tiny ceramic vegetables (leeks, cauliflowers, and eggplants). Embroidery, sewn to look like jewelry, adorned the neckline of certain items of clothing. She used clips inspired by the fastenings on French mechanics' overalls; buttons in the shape of padlocks or musical notes; gold coins strung on a grosgrain ribbon around the neck.

Elsa Schiaparelli's original ideas were so numerous and innovative that they are still inspiring to today's couturières.

SURREALISM: jewelry AS A symbol

As you become older, art and life become one and the same.

—GEORGES BRAQUE

Sketch of Dali's telephone earring design.

The original Surrealist artists of the '40s and '50s were inspired by the growing interest in psychology and Sigmund Freud's writings on the unconscious, the importance of dreams, and symbols. These kinds of metaphorical references lent themselves well to jewelry, which is a symbolic medium itself. Moreover, most of the symbols used by the Surrealist painters were perfect for jewelry: butterflies to symbolize metamorphosis or birdcages to symbolize imprisonment and freedom. Eyes, lips, and hands were popular symbols, too. No wonder so many twentieth-century artists and sculptors, including Jean Arp, Georges Braque, Jean Cocteau, Max Ernst, Jean Clement, Man Ray, Yves Tanguy, Alexander Calder, and Jean Dubuffet, tried their hand at designing jewelry.

THE FUTURE: wearable art AND technology

In the '90s, advances in technological devices made cell phones the new hip accessories. Now, in this millennium, major technology companies are hiring fashion consultants and offering new models for each season, much as the big fashion houses do. And they are thinking more and more about wearable technology rather than just portable gadgets—soon tech accessories will go way beyond, say, a leopard-print phone to match your shoes. Cell phones will become more like computers, and better speech recognition software might make keypads obsolete. Already some cell phones, audio players, and digital cameras are small enough to be worn around the neck, and there are sunglasses with built-in display screens, portable computer backup memory rods, and the multitasking Apple iPhone.

A fashion that does not reach the streets is not a fashion.
—COCO CHANEL

And it's not only about communication. More and more we'll be wearing accessories that "do" something beyond just looking good. The future also promises jewelry that is useful as well as meaningful. An Australian company has brought out a wristband bracelet that changes color as UV levels rise, alerting the wearer when it's time to apply sunscreen. An Alaskan company has come up with a ring that contains a microchip programmed to heat up the day before an anniversary. Cosmetic companies have begun to make bracelets and pendants to contain makeup. Banks issue mini–credit cards that can be worn as jewelry. And Nokia is developing a medallion e-necklace to which users can upload images to be displayed on the necklace pendant.

Of course, this isn't junk jewelry. But it is part of the trend toward wearing accessories that are not just beautiful, but expressions of who we are and what we find meaningful.

Junk jewelry idea taken from a **Man Ray** photograph of champagne cork earrings made by the artist **Meret Oppenheim,** circa 1950.

PART | ②

CONCEPT-UALIZING

IN THIS KIND OF JEWELRY, THE IDEA IS THE PART THAT'S VALUABLE. THE "JUNK" IN JUNK JEWELRY IS CHOSEN FOR ITS WIT OR ITS ASSOCIATIONS—WHICH TURN IT INTO SOMETHING MORE VALUABLE THAN JUNK.

THINKING like an artist

The essence of all art is to have pleasure in giving pleasure.

—MIKHAIL BARYSHNIKOV

How do artists know whether their scribbles have created a work of art worth thousands of dollars—or whether they have merely ruined an expensive piece of drawing paper? When you are making junk jewelry, how do you know whether you've made something stylish and hip—or a big, fat mess, reminiscent of an amateurish children's craft project?

Although jaded professional artists will tell you that a piece of art is worth nothing until a patron pays for it, people are usually drawn to a work either because they find it pleasing to the eye or because the subject matter interests them, or both.

In other words, if a piece is put together in a way that makes the viewer enjoy looking at it, it works. If it sends a message that evokes a response in your audience, it also works. Prose is just a string of words until a reader relates to it in some way; a painting is just a collection of brushstrokes until it resonates with meaning for the person who studies it.

If you make things that are both visually and intellectually intriguing (even if you make them just for yourself), the effort will be worthwhile.

But I'm not an artist!

Translating your idea of what you want to make into reality in a way that the viewer immediately understands and appreciates may take a lot of trial and error. It can be frustrating when something doesn't turn out the way you've imagined it in your mind's eye. But for those who enjoy the challenge, it's as addictive as crossword puzzles.

There will be times when you doubt your ability to create something nice enough to wear. At those times, ponder these thoughts:

Tiny brushes from makeup palettes make nifty "artistic" earrings and a mini paint pot tray makes a cute pendant.

- **THERE ARE HUNDREDS OF DIFFERENT ARTISTIC STYLES** in museums, from abstract to hyperrealism. We take it for granted that the people who developed these styles are talented. But what makes these artists' ways of expressing themselves any more valid than yours?

- **IF YOU CAN ENJOY THE MAKING OF SOMETHING WHILE YOU ARE DOING IT**—solving the little problems of "would that look better here or there" to your own satisfaction—jewelry-making will not be a waste of time, whatever the result.

- **YOU MAY LIKE WHAT YOU'VE MADE TODAY AND HATE IT TOMORROW.** With junk jewelry, you can wear a piece for a while and then you can change it. There is no stability in life, and that can be a very liberating thought when it comes to fashioning your own look. Add more elements, then take some away. Definitions of what is finished and complete are totally fluid. Follow your ideas wherever they take you.

- Machine-made jewelry may be constructed more neatly, but **THINGS THAT ARE HAND-CRAFTED ARE USUALLY MORE INHERENTLY VALUABLE.**

- **IF YOU END UP WITH SOMETHING YOU DON'T LIKE, CONSIDER IT AN EXERCISE OR AN EXPERIMENT.** Making things that you never doubted would succeed is as meaningless as flipping a coin that is the same on both sides.

- **ONE FRIEND MAY HATE WHAT YOU'VE DONE WHILE ANOTHER MIGHT LOVE IT.** Everyone has particular preferences and opinions. There are no immutable laws when it comes to art and craft. If you can shift your perspective so you are unconcerned about whether anyone else will appreciate what you've made, you'll free yourself to play, to enjoy making something.

- **IN ART, THERE ARE NO INEFFECTUAL ELEMENTS, ONLY INEFFECTUAL ARTISTS.** In other words, it's what you do with what you have that transforms your piece into something wearable. Whatever materials you use are fine. In this kind of art, workmanship is generally less important than how you use your imagination.

There are two ways to approach junk jewelry-making: You can start by thinking up ways to make the detritus of modern life into something wonderful—that is, by transforming the things you come across serendipitously. Or, you can begin by making a list of what you want to symbolize. If, for example, you are creating a "trashy treasure" that aims to sum up who you are as a person, think back on the high points in your life—cities you've visited, favorite foods or hobbies, things you adore or detest. Then look for small items that symbolize those experiences—miniature doll shoes if you have shoe-a-holic tendencies, a guitar pick if you love music, charms to represent a city that captivates you.

If there's a particular kind of store you love to wander in—whether it's a hardware, stationery, or dime store—pay it a visit with a whole new "eye" and try to visualize how what you see on the store shelves could become neat jewelry.

Draw Inspiration from Jewelry Designers

There are a number of contemporary designers who are creating inspiring work. These are just a few of the designers who use unusual or everyday found objects to make jewelry.

Only those who will risk going too far can possibly find out how far one can go.
—T. S. ELLIOT

UGO CORREANI began designing jewelry in Milan in 1973 and has worked with Gianni Versace and Karl Lagerfeld. His junk jewelry designs include a showerhead necklace and newspaper bracelets and, with Karl Lagerfeld for Chloé, a piano keyboard choker.

TOM BINNS was born in Ireland and lives in Manhattan. He has worked with Miuccia Prada and Narciso Rodriguez, designed for Vivienne Westwood's collections, and worked with Comme des Garçons. Items he has used in his designs include clothespins, safety pins, Mickey Mouse badges, newspapers, and popsicle sticks. He has also made bent-fork bracelets and pen-nib brooches.

Australian fashion designer MICHELLE JANK uses the jewelry, laces, and textiles she finds in antique and secondhand shops as starting points. Her tiaras, anklets, earrings, and charm bracelets feature key tags, ring pulls from cans, glass, chains, buckles, and zippers. Some of her pieces were used in the final season of the TV show *Sex and the City.*

TATTY DEVINE, a company started by Harriet Vine and Rosie Wolfenden in 2001, is famous for its quirky accessories, which, as noted on the company website, elevate jewelry to an art status. They sell items such as potato-chip necklaces, price-ticket cuff links, and music-note bracelets. Stella McCartney is said to be a fan of their work.

JUDY BLAME, A.K.A. CHRIS BARNES, is an English designer who has worked with Boy George and Rei Kawakubo of Comme des Garçons. His work has incorporated medallions of saints, shells, ID tags, buttons, string, safety pins, rubber bands, badges, feathers, champagne corks, paper clips, pill bottles, stamps, hammer heads, crosses, buttons, stars, shells, and plastic six-pack holders.

ARTISTIC techniques

To give you some ideas about how to create junk jewelry that's both great-looking and clever, and to make it more likely that you'll have fun rather than frustration in the process, here is a mix of visual and conceptual ways to assemble art. They are the tools artists and craftspeople use to make compositions visually and intellectually appealing. These techniques are borrowed from artists, sculptors, designers, and photo stylists.

Artistic Technique #1:
ELEVATE THE MUNDANE TO ART STATUS BY ISOLATING IT

It's magic: Anything you place in a frame or on a pedestal, or enclose alone in a glass case, instantly turns into art. By showcasing an object, you are effectively marking it as something special, to which attention must be paid.

The more ordinary and everyday the object, the more dissonance you create by highlighting it. The Dada artist Marcel Duchamp was one of the first artists to explore these kinds of transformations: He signed a urinal and exhibited it in an art gallery—instant shock value. The artist Claes Oldenburg used scale to achieve the same effect: He has created huge versions of ordinary objects, such as apple cores, safety pins, binoculars, and hamburgers. Andy Warhol painted mundane Campbell's soup cans.

In the same way that anything with a frame around it becomes art, anything you choose to wear as jewelry becomes jewelry. By putting an object in the place where, traditionally, a valuable stone such as a diamond would be worn, you are automatically elevating the object's status and making a comment on its worth. This raises some provocative questions in the viewer's mind: Is this valuable? And, if so, why?

However, if you haven't isolated the object effectively, then you won't have achieved "art" status. A candy wrapper pinned to a dress with a safety pin looks like a mistake—but that same candy wrapper encased in rigid plastic, or enlarged or

To make these earrings, shorten the blunt end of a pencil to the desired length by using a carving knife or making a clean cut with a craft knife. Glue on an "up eye," which is basically a tiny flat disc with a jump ring attached to it. Add an earring hook and you're done.

otherwise treated as something special, makes a statement. By drawing attention to a particular object using a method that is usually reserved for rare gems or precious metals, you are inviting your audience to look carefully at your selection and to ponder its significance.

Artistic Technique #2:
BRING TOGETHER TWO CONNECTED IDEAS TO MAKE A WITTY COMMENTARY

The most amusing junk jewelry makes a visual pun—multiple associations are united in one concept or symbol. When Dali made telephone earrings, he created both a visual pun (ear, rings) as well as a visual surprise. Using sea shells as the ear pieces for headphones (an idea several people have come up with) brings to mind the childhood game of listening to the sound of the sea through a shell and makes a sly statement about technology and nature. Using a tape measure as a belt pokes fun at our obsession with weight loss.

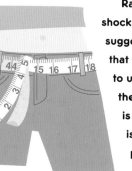

Rather than simply using something crazy for its own sake, or merely for shock value, take advantage of these kinds of connections. Use a symbol that suggests two or more different meanings. Try to create multiple associations that resonate as a single concept. Take time to think about an item you want to use before you do anything with it. What does it remind you of? Are there different connotations associated with its name? What other objects is it similar to in shape or color? What could it be used in place of? That is, does its form lend itself to use in an unusual way—could you use it in place of a belt buckle or a button or an eyeglass lanyard? Is it a metaphor for something else?

Threading a tape measure through the belt loops around your jeans makes fun of the whole idea of "watching your weight."

Artistic Technique #3:
GROUP MUNDANE THINGS TOGETHER

From a distance, necklaces or bracelets made of stationery clips, saftey pins, or other small, mundane items do not "read" as clips or pins. We don't recognize these homely items for what they are. In fact, observers are usually entranced when they recognize they have been "tricked" in much the same way that trompe l'oeil paintings fool the eye.

When you take simple items and mass many of them together, the whole becomes, visually, something quite different than the sum of its parts. Anything that is small and cheap and that has an interesting shape can be used this way: paper clips, bobby pins, buttons.

Artistic Technique #4:
ASSEMBLE INGREDIENTS WITH A THEME IN MIND

The "charm necklace" below derives its allure from the sheer number of elements incorporated in it. And because all the items are similar in color, mainly yellow and orange, it has something of a conventional look. The humor comes from the sheer exuberance of its summertime-at-the-beach theme and the juxtaposition of the mundane (flip-flop sandals) and the silly (lobsters) with the pretty (shells). Another example of a theme might be the Wild West: You could collect tiny wagon wheels, cowboy boots, hats, pistols, and sheriff's badges, to fashion an Annie Oakley–style bracelet or necklace.

This type of assemblage looks as if it would be simple to construct, but typically much trial and error is involved. As with making patchwork quilts or decorating a room, you need to do a lot of mixing and matching and eliminating to get a collection of items that ultimately works well together. But it's the collecting and playing around with quirky little objects that's the fun part of creating junk jewelry.

Chain made by joining brass snap swivels (used for fishing) with jump rings.

Choose a theme and gather together as many small objects as possible that relate to it. Attach each one to a chain with links large enough to take the connecting jump ring.

And bear in mind that junk jewelry is sometimes best made not from an actual piece of junk, but from a plastic version that makes reference to it. Using a real fish skeleton as part of a necklace sends a message, certainly, but wearing a stylish, graphic depiction of a fish skeleton better focuses attention on the symbolism of what you are wearing instead of the smelly reality.

Artistic Technique #5:
FOR UNITY, GROUP BY COLOR, SHAPE, OR TEXTURE

When you group together a number of things that all have a similar color or texture or shape, you are creating a visually pleasing whole. Our brains are constantly striving to make sense of the world by discerning patterns, and grouping similar objects as units transforms previously isolated items into an artistic assemblage, or pattern.

By virtue of the unusual grouping, the viewer is invited to consider similarities in shape and to look at a mundane object in a different way.

If you have a number of items you want to use, but they don't seem to work well together, consider spray-painting them all one color to give them a unified look.

Different types of household laundry pins in shades of blue bound together with blue wire.

Artistic Technique #6:
CREATE RHYTHM BY CONTRASTING SHAPE

A series of objects has a visual rhythm in the same way that music has an audible rhythm. This rhythm is created by repetition and variation. While simple repetition of one shape is soothing and calming and unifies the elements, it is boring without variation. By using contrasting shapes and uneven spaces, you create drama and edginess.

As you transform your junk into jewelry, use rhythm to make crazy things calmer or ordinary things visually stimulating. To take the edge off really wacky objects, use

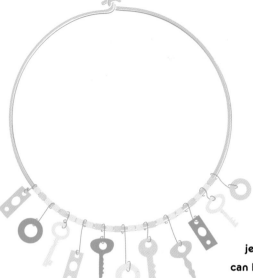

them as if they were elements of traditional jewelry with carefully ordered rhythms. At the other extreme—to make banal objects more exciting—create unusual spacing for a syncopated rhythm. For example, vary the spaces between strung beads by varying the placement of the knots. The "empty spaces" between elements play a part, too. Artists call the area between two objects a negative shape, and that negative can be just as powerful as a positive shape. The closer two elements are, the more tension there is between them.

Artistic Technique #7:
THINK OF WIRE AS A MEDIUM WITH WHICH TO DRAW

Wire is a wonderful medium. Armed with nothing more than a pair of round-nosed pliers, you can make all sorts of curlicues and spirals and three-dimensional doodles out of it. Try it!

Some of the best colored wire comes from telephone cable—next time you see an electrician working with this wire, ask if he or she has any spare off-cuts available.

For inspiration, look at the jewelry of Alexander Calder. He was primarily a sculptor, famous for his "mobiles" and "stabiles," but he did make jewelry for friends. Some of his pieces include found objects, such as bits of bones, uncut stones, and glass, but most are made from twisted gold, silver, or brass wire. These pieces exude a wonderful spirit of freedom and energy—line drawings made solid. Look, too, at the

The lightweight elements used here were found in a toolbox and attached to the neck ring with wire of various lengths. The "spacers" are short, curled lengths of metal snipped from brass fasteners [the kind of clips used to keep hole-punched papers together].

The owner of these antique fish-shaped game pieces wanted to wear them (she's a Pisces!), but she didn't want to disfigure them in any way. Solution: Use wire to create a "net" to hold them gently. A brooch pin is attached to the wire at the back.

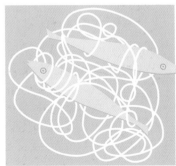

The simple circular
paperclip (common
in Europe) becomes,
through repetition,
an elegant chain.

When you find an
object like the
whistle to the
right—something
that is handmade
with an elegant
form and a dis-
tressed metal
surface—you need
to do nothing more
than wear it
on a cord.

drawings of the late Saul Steinberg, whose art ap-
peared often in the *New Yorker* magazine, to see
how line can suggest all sorts of ideas, including words and feelings and emotion.

Artistic Technique #8:
CELEBRATE A QUALITY BY REPETITION

Repetition is often used in conventional
jewelry—a string of pearls, multiple bracelets,
matching sets. You can make a very subtle piece of
junk jewelry this way: Anything with a hole becomes
a bead when it is threaded. Anything that can be linked
becomes a chain. Anything that comes in several different
colors can be put together to show off complementary hues.

Also, think about whether your piece should be
symmetrical, that is, if one side should mirror the other.
This is the traditional, conservative look of jewelry. Asymmetrical groupings are informal, surprising, and quirky.

Artistic Technique #9:
LET A PLEASING OBJECT BE ITSELF

Some of the most striking junk jewelry uses an item just as it is,
especially when that item possesses its own aesthetically pleasing
attributes. A sculptural shape or timeworn texture is inherently beautiful. The Japanese have a term for the beautiful imperfections age and
weather bring about: wabi sabi. By choosing to wear something like this,
you are highlighting its uniqueness, honoring the story it has to tell.

But if you feel you must do something more, let the object inspire the
setting. Highlight, for example, the beautiful shape of an item by hanging it upside down so that the first impression the viewer registers is the

silhouette of the object, rather than what it actually is. Or, if you want to emphasize texture, play that up by placing the object on something with a contrasting texture—a rusted key against a plain white square of plastic, for example.

Artistic Technique #10:
WHAT DOES IT REMIND YOU OF?

Found something unusual that you want to use as jewelry? What does it remind you of? Try nudging it toward that incarnation. If you see something in a hardware store that suggests to you a metal ring designed by an avant-garde jeweler, wear it as a ring, even though, technically, the packaging says it's called a Clip Hose Worm Drive! (Cigar bands and knitters' plastic stitch counters make neat rings, too.)

Blurring the edges between what a thing is and what it looks like can create interesting shifts in perspective.

Or you can take your inspiration from "real" jewelry and apparel. You could make your own version of an Elizabethan ruff out of newspaper, for example. Or make the equivalent of an African neckpiece using old forks and spoons instead of carved beads.

These small rubber lizards bring to mind jeweled pins in the shape of iguanas. It was easy to join the lizards claw to claw with instant glue, and since the tails already curved, they are easily formed into loops.

PART | ③

> Fashion is not something that exists in dresses only. Fashion is in the sky, in the street, fashion has to do with ideas, the way we live, what is happening.
>
> **—COCO CHANEL**

Imagination IS MORE IMPORTANT THAN KNOWLEDGE. —Albert Einstein

CREATING

HUNTING GROUNDS |

HOW TO | ?

design ideas | 💡

Raw Materials | 🚚

Successful junk jewelry is both art and craft.

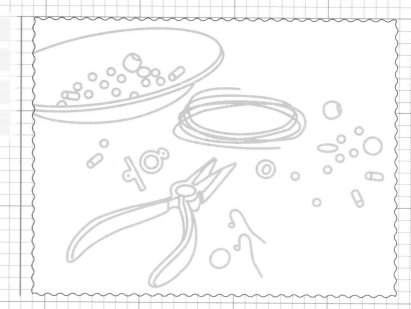

STARTING the pack rat WAY

If you are the sort of person who admires junk jewelry, you probably already collect things that interest you. Perhaps you spend hours at flea markets and yard sales looking for quirky stuff, or you regularly go on dime-store spending sprees. If that's the case, you may already have a collection of costume jewelry that can be disassembled, ransacked for "parts," or updated with new and different doodads. (However, never pull apart real gold or silver jewelry to do this! It would be a horrible shame to ruin a valuable or antique piece to make something ephemeral.)

And remember, the whole point of junk jewelry is to use found objects creatively—so if you can't afford to buy a lot of parts and tools, improvise.

For example, for an easy way to join a necklace at the back of the neck, check for any easy-to-bend wire that may be lying around the house, or see if you can beg some florist wire from a local florist or floral designer. With this wire, using pliers and a wire cutter, make a fishhook shape as shown above. A large jump ring on the other end of a necklace is all you need to create an effective clasp.

In fact, you may not need a fastener at all. A few inches (cm) of ribbon attached to each end of the necklace and tied in a bow makes an avant-garde closure. And consider some of these alternative materials you could use to wear things around your neck: leather thongs (don't throw away that old suede tie or handbag—cut it into strips!); keyring-chain-type ball chain; old chains you already have; colored telephone wire; yarn; braid; rope; shoelaces; clear fishing line (for an "invisible"

Look for a set of miniature pencils, or use stubs of regular colored pencils, to make this necklace. Either drill a hole through each one, or glue an up ring to each side. Join with jump rings and chain.

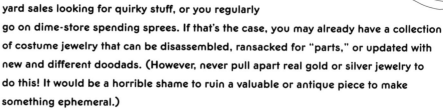

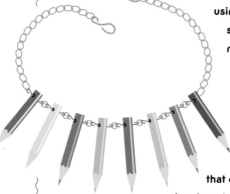

effect); elastic thread; hemp; satin cord; elastic string; the plastic chain that eyeglass lanyard cords are sometimes made of; or a single rigid circle of wire around the neck.

But do give some thought to what the most complementary addition would be. For example, if you're using brightly colored keytags, you might string them on a colorful plastic chain. Try a few different materials until you get the hanging element that looks as if it were meant expressly for what you want to hang from it.

RAW MATERIALS: finding

Findings are what jewelers call the bits and pieces that actually do the work—the loops of wire that hold the "jewel" in the ear, the brooch pin that connects the glitz to your clothing, the clasp that turns a string of beads into a necklace.

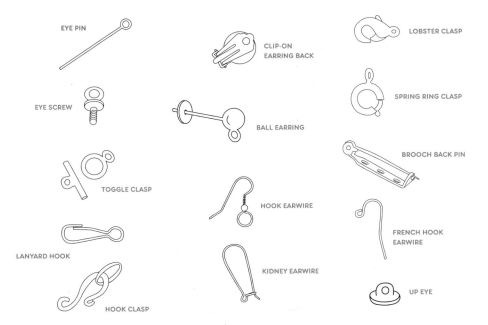

EYE PIN

CLIP-ON EARRING BACK

LOBSTER CLASP

EYE SCREW

BALL EARRING

SPRING RING CLASP

BROOCH BACK PIN

TOGGLE CLASP

HOOK EARWIRE

FRENCH HOOK EARWIRE

LANYARD HOOK

KIDNEY EARWIRE

UP EYE

HOOK CLASP

Your local hobby shop or even the local dime store may carry findings, but for a huge selection, go online. It's easy to find sites that stock a good variety of findings in different finishes and price ranges. They also have glues and wire and tools.

In fact, you may be overwhelmed at first: Which style should you choose? Which are best—barrel clasps, spring-lock clasps, or lobster clasps? Ideally, the attachment element should coordinate well with the rest of the piece in terms of finish, size, and shape. (Finish refers to the color of the findings. They may look like silver or gold, but cheaper findings are usually made of brass, steel, or zinc coated with nickel, copper, or gilt, to give them the look of more expensive metals. Some are dipped in an oxide solution for a dark, "antique" appearance.)

If you use "silver" jump rings, you should use a "silver" finish earring wire. And if you are making a necklace that is small and delicate, you should use a small, unobtrusive necklace clasp. However, brooch backs are hidden against your clothes and necklace closures will be at the back of your neck, so don't worry too much about aesthetics to begin with, especially while you are experimenting. If you create something you really love, you can replace your improvised fastenings with the ideal findings later on.

BARE necessities

Jump rings—tiny circles of rigid wire that jewelers use to join different elements—are a must. Five or 6 millimeters is a good size to begin with. The right way to open jump rings is to bend them apart sideways, so the ring retains its circular shape. If you pull the two ends away from each other into a U shape, it's difficult to get the jump ring to meet together again without a gap.

You will need two pairs of pliers to open jump rings, but there may already be at least one pair in the family toolbox. If you want to work with wire, you'll also need wire cutters, which you may already have at home as well. Your pliers might have a section

THE VOICE OF EXPERIENCE

Since this kind of jewelry is (the name gives you a clue here!) junk, it's okay to use glue to bond objects together rather than welding them. But to avoid lost attachments and disappointment, you should always try to use the right kind of glue. There are many different types of adhesives available because there is no one perfect glue for everything—and they each have advantages and disadvantages. To choose the most suitable glue, know what kind of surfaces you are trying to bond and read the label on the glue packet carefully, or check with a knowledgeable hardware-store salesperson.

The two best glues for junk jewelry-making, where you are usually joining small bits of plastic and metal, are probably superglue and epoxy resin glue. Superglue or Krazy glue (Cyanoacrylate adhesive) comes in tiny tubes. Epoxy resin glue is the kind where you have to mix part A with part B. Both make a very strong bond, but they each have drawbacks.

. . . it's what you do with what you have that transforms it into something wearable

two parts is fiddly, and the glue cures very quickly, which means you only have a few minutes to use it. And some types can turn yellowish after a while.

Superglue is brittle and can shatter easily if the bond gets banged. It can also mar a clear surface, such as plastic, and make it cloudy. (It's good, though, for sealing a knot of thread.) Epoxy resin glue can only be used on surfaces that are clean and free of grease. Mixing the

Add a jump ring to get the hanging part facing the way you want.

with a sharp edge for cutting wire. Round-nosed pliers are invaluable for working with wire, too, in order to get curves rather than angles.

If all the tools you have on hand are large, it's a good idea to buy a pair of very small pliers. The ones small enough to fit comfortably in your palm and with a delicate little "nose" tiny enough to fit inside a jump ring are a joy to use and easy to maneuver.

A craft knife (the sort with blades that you can snap off when they become blunt) is very useful, too.

The ideal way to make holes in small objects is to use a cordless rotary tool like a Dremel tool. However, the kind of hand tool that is designed for creating holes for screws will often work on soft materials like plastic.

THE **HOW-TO** projects

Someday all department stores will become museums, and all museums will become department stores.

—ANDY WARHOL

Here are guidelines on how to make a number of pieces from "junk" that is not too hard to find. Remember, the fun of making junk jewelry has to do with serendipity, innovation, and creativity. We've provided notes about the "hunting grounds" you can explore for particular pieces. While you're there, you might find other things that are entirely different and more exciting: Go with them!

If what you make doesn't work when you put it on, nevermind! Wear it for a day, and if you feel silly, give it to a five-year-old (but only, of course, if there are no parts that could be swallowed or otherwise cause damage). This is ephemeral stuff. If you enjoy fiddling around with jump rings and junk and want to go further, learn how to weld metals properly. Consider *Junk Jewelry* as an introductory course to get a feel for making jewelry.

MIX AND MATCH OUTRAGEOUS ODDS AND ENDS FOR A TRULY UNIQUE LOOK.

THE TRASHY Treasure NECKLACE

MAKE A THREE-DIMENSIONAL SCRAPBOOK TO WEAR!

HUNTING GROUNDS

This is the ideal final resting place for any TINY MEMENTO that is too significant to throw away—the kind of **useless bits and pieces** that end up at the bottom of a dressing-table drawer: your grandmother's watch that doesn't work, the ring you never wear, the tiny plastic pig that your first boyfriend gave you, orphan earrings. To make a "This is your life" kind of necklace for a friend, take notes on her *loves* (shoes, music) and *hates* (licorice candy) and use them to assemble a QUIRKY collection of tiny items that represent facets of who she is. Hobby shops that sell dollhouse supplies are a good resource.

> **THIS**
> IS THE IDEAL FINAL RESTING PLACE FOR ANY TINY MEMENTO THAT IS TOO SIGNIFICANT TO THROW AWAY.

Raw Materials

You'll need to find a way to attach these treasures to a chain. Things that **already have holes** in them are easy to attach with jump rings. Otherwise, you can either DRILL A HOLE, GLUE ON AN UP EYE, screw in a screw eye, or WRAP WIRE around the "jewel." The method you choose depends on what the thing is made of, how big it is, and how much you want to mess with it.

design ideas

① Make use of what you have, and see if a theme emerges, whether that theme is "jewelry I used to wear as a teenager" or "souvenirs from my trip to Paris." If you inherited Grandma's cheap costume jewelry box or your father's fishing tackle box, combine elements to make a necklace or pin to recall and honor that person. ② You can mix and match plastic with trash, and disregard proportions—the more crowded and busy, the better.

HOW TO | ?

Use a chain with large links so that you can attach each item to a different link and space out the objects in a way that looks good. Or go for excess and crowd on as much as you can. (But even if you do this, try to distribute the colors evenly and keep sizes balanced.)

Place the items on a flat surface first, and arrange them until you have a pleasing combination of shapes and colors. If you need a long shape at the front, but don't have anything the right length, thread a bead on a short piece of wire and twist each end into a loop.

Make sure you attach each item to the bottom of the link so it falls freely.

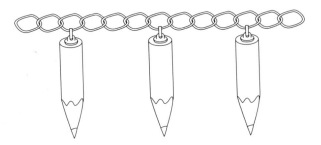

Keep all the items hanging from the same part of the link, as above, or they will not hang well.

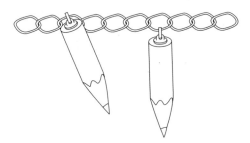

A BEAUTIFUL BRASS FITTING, ORIGINALLY MADE TO COVER THE KEY AND HANDLE OPENINGS OF A DOOR. A METAL PAPER
FASTENER WAS THREADED THROUGH THE SCREW HOLE AT THE TOP AND TWISTED TO MAKE A LOOP SO THE FITTING COULD HANG
FROM A BRASS NECK RING.

ANTIQUE hardware bodywear

WEAR A LITTLE BIT OF ANTIQUE FURNITURE.

HUNTING GROUNDS

Have you recently passed by some furniture that was being thrown out on the street? Look for drawer pulls and metal fittings—sometimes they're all that's worth saving. Search for interesting old bits of ANTIQUE HARDWARE and the detailed workmanship of years gone by in industrial antique stores or on websites that carry reproductions.

FREQUENT
TAG SALES AND BROWSE AMONG THE BITS AND PIECES IN THOSE DOZENS OF BABY-FOOD JARS IN YOUR DAD'S OR GRANDFATHER'S WORKSHOP

Raw Materials

Years ago, furniture makers put a lot of thought into details such as **furniture hardware**—this necklace pays homage to those dedicated craftspeople. In the old days, hardware was made of quality metals, like brass, which polish up beautifully. Try cleaning a little bit with an **ALL-PURPOSE METAL CLEANER** to see if a piece you've found takes on a glow.

design idea

Anyone who works at fixing old things—watch and clock makers, furniture upholsterers, locksmiths—might have something perfect for a piece of junk jewelry among his or her discards.

HOW TO | ?

It took just seconds to make the piece shown below. This brass drawer pull came from an antique drawer that escaped the trash heap because it was used as a storage box in a workshop. It was teamed up with some matching chain that echoed the corkscrew detail on the pull itself. The chain was attached to the drawer pull with a jump ring at one end and a spring-lock clasp at the other. Cleaning up the hardware with lots of brass cleaner took much longer, but it was a labor of love.

For wearable art, look for old things with a pleasing shape, a weathered patina, or symbolic meaning.

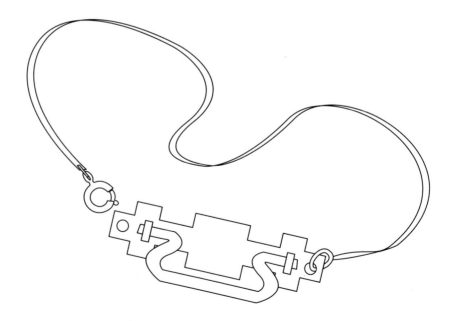

THE SURREALISTS OFTEN USED DRAWERS AS A SYMBOL OF A PERSON'S INNER DEPTHS.

ODDS AND ENDS OF CHAIN MAKE FOR A KINETIC HANGING CHAIN NECKLACE.

HANGING chain necklace

THINK YOUR BROKEN NECKLACE CHAINS ARE USELESS? THINK AGAIN!

HUNTING GROUNDS

GATHER ANY SPARE BITS OF CHAIN in your jewelry box or tool box. Combine these bits with chain from a **HARDWARE** or **BEAD** store.

MIX UP
SILVER, GOLD, AND STEEL FOR A FUNKY, URBAN EDGE.

Raw Materials

Work with chains of the same metal for a chic monochromatic look or mix up silver, gold, and steel for a funky, urban edge. Purchase a sleek neck ring from a jewelry-supply shop to tie the whole look together.

design ideas

① Create an asymmetrical shape by starting with the longest chains first and ending with the shortest, or place the longer chains in the middle for a sleek V-shape. ② Hook a few lengths of chain on a couple of earwires for funky dangle earrings.

HOW TO ?

The easiest way to work is to thread the chain on the neck ring, varying the weights and colors next to each other. (We used about 25 pieces in this example.) Add a jump ring to the wire if the links are too small to thread on the neck wire. When you're done, take a wire cutter and give the chain fringe a "haircut" at various lengths, as your sense of style dictates.

Clamp a jump ring tightly around ball chain to make a loop in it.

THE TWO DIFFERENT KINDS OF CLIPS USED HERE SHOW OFF THE GREAT CLIP COLORS THAT ARE AVAILABLE.

STYLISH COLLAR OR OFFICE JUNK?
IT'S ALL IN THE EYE OF THE BEHOLDER.

HUNTING GROUNDS

STATIONERY-SUPPLY STORES are a treasure trove of assorted clips designed to keep papers together. They come in all different colors, shapes, and SIZES. (If you travel abroad, look for **unusual paper clip** styles in other countries. In foreign stationery stores you'll discover lots of practical gifts for the folks back home, as well as "jewelry" supplies.)

Raw Materials

In the larger stationery stores and on the Internet, you'll find **bulldog clips**—also known as foldback clips—in an array of colors. For a necklace, find the SMALLEST SIZE, which is probably about half an inch (13mm) long.

design idea

Stationery stores have many other items that would make great "jewelry," too: brass pen nibs, pens on string to wear around your neck, miniature pencils, cardboard tags, and labels.

HOW TO

The "silver" handles on bulldog clips will come off if you squeeze the two sides in together toward each other and ease them out one side at a time. To make a neckpiece, you will need about twenty half-inch (13mm) clips. Detach the handles from one side of each clip. In the spaces where the handles were, thread a length of fabric-covered elastic. Make a knot and hide it inside the nearest clip. If you wish, detach the clips from the other side of each clip as well.

Squeeze the sides of the clips to detach.

Thread elastic cord through empty tunnels.

REMOVE THE CLIP HANDLES OR NOT, AS YOU CHOOSE.

YOU'LL NEED A LOT OF THEM, BUT THREADED FLAT, BUTTONS MAKE GREAT BEADS.

BUTTON BRILLIANCE

THE HUMBLE BUTTON MAKES AN ELEGANT FLAT BEAD.

HUNTING GROUNDS

Find common or garden-variety plastic buttons in **GRANDMA'S BUTTON BOX**, at button shops or sewing-supply stores (where you'll sometimes find cheap buttons sold in bulk, by the scoop), and at **thrift shops** and yard sales. You can even hunt for **INTERESTING BUTTONS** in your closet. Combine buttons from clothing or coats you're no longer wearing with store-bought buttons for an **ECLECTIC** look.

Raw Materials

This necklace was made by gathering many **variations on "white" buttons** (that is, buttons that vary from matte plastic to faux mother of pearl), plus a few clear, pink, darker beige, tortoiseshell, and brown ones as well. Using **GRADATIONS OF ONE COLOR** (all kinds of blue buttons, for example, from baby blue to aquamarine to royal blue) will give a more sophisticated look while using a variety of colors will give you a funkier look.

BUTTONS CAN BE THREADED EITHER FLAT OR STACKED

design ideas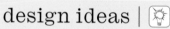

① Buttons can be threaded either flat or stacked. If you stack them so that only the edges show—as is done here—you'll get a subtle piece that looks more like a necklace of flat onyx beads than buttons. This necklace took about 225 buttons. ② If you don't have enough, you could always use regular round beads interspersed between the buttons.

HOW TO ?

Spread out the buttons on a table roughly according to size, using the smallest for the back of the neck and the largest at the front. If you use a combination of four-holed buttons and two-holed buttons, as we did, you'll get a slightly off-center gradation. Using all of one sort makes for a more uniformly graded necklace.

Take a piece of white elastic thread at least twice as long as you want the necklace to be. It helps to tease out the fabric covering a little on each end of the elastic and dab these threads with clear nail polish or instant glue and pull them into a point. That way you'll have a built-in "needle" to help thread the buttons. The easiest way of working is to thread the biggest ones first, to get the important central part of the necklace established the way you want it. Then add smaller buttons to each end of the elastic so you can judge as you go whether each side more or less matches. When all the buttons are on and just the way you want them, tie a knot in one end of the elastic and pass the other end back through the buttons, using the free hole on two-hole buttons and either an adjacent hole on four-hole buttons (for an uneven gradation) or the diametrically opposite hole (for a more even graduation).

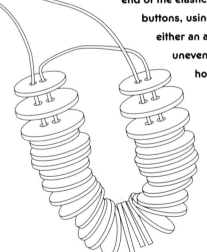

When the thread has been passed through this second time, pull the elastic until all the buttons fit snugly together. Tie a knot. If the knot is near a four-hole button, you may be able to conceal the ends by poking them though a spare hole.

Thread the buttons twice, like this, for a secure necklace.

YOU NEED ONLY A FEW UNUSUAL BUTTONS FOR THIS LOOK.

More BUTTON BRILLIANCE

VARY THE WAY YOU THREAD A BUTTON TO MAKE THE MOST OF IT.

HUNTING GROUNDS

Look for **UNUSUAL BUTTONS** at specialty **button shops,** sewing-supply stores, or antiques shops, or cut them from **OLD CLOTHING** that you are about to throw away.

BUTTONS MEANT FOR CHILDREN'S CLOTHES COME IN FUN SHAPES . . .

Buttons meant for *children's clothes* come in fun shapes, such as animals, letters, toys, and sports equipment.

HOW TO

These flower-shaped buttons were threaded onto pliable white wire to keep them in place. While flower shapes are cute, you could use any type of button for this style of necklace. (Buttons that have shanks—that is, the fastening hole is hidden at the back—can be strung, but it's difficult to make them stay in place.)

Raw Materials

When you **USE WIRE** to thread buttons, you have more control—it's easier to make them stay where you want them. But a bracelet is usually more comfortable to wear when the basis is **elastic thread**.

design idea

When you find one or more buttons you want to use, either because they are unusual or they feature a color you like, tape them to a small piece of cardboard and carry them with you. Whenever you pass a store that may have buttons or beads that will work well with them, just whip out your buttons and compare.

HOW TO | ?

Find seven large buttons (1 inch [2.5cm] in diameter) and seven smaller buttons of a different color that will fit well with the larger buttons. Use fabric-covered elastic to thread the buttons, as shown. Pull the elastic tight, so that the buttons overlap a little, and knot.

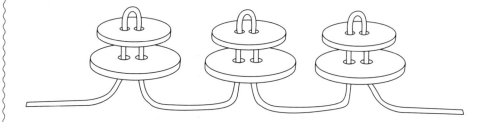

Thread buttons with fabric-covered elastic for a bracelet.

FOR THIS TYPE OF BRACELET, EXPERIMENT UNTIL YOU FIND TWO SIZES OF BUTTONS THAT FIT WELL TOGETHER, THEN STRING THEM WITH ELASTIC THREAD.

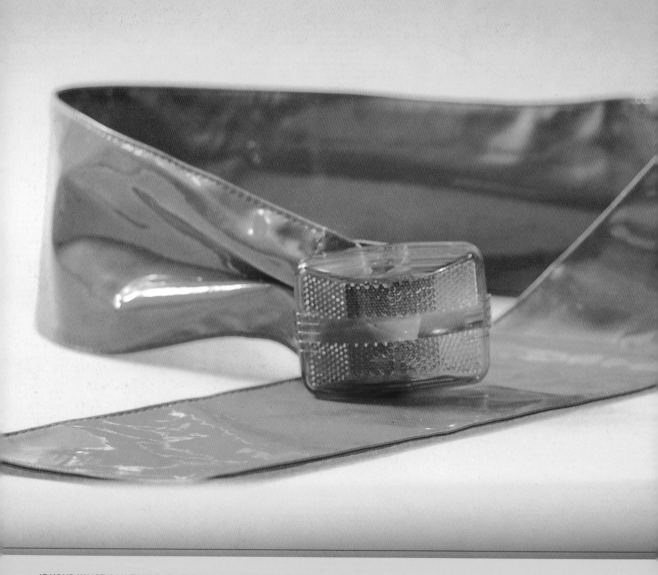

IF YOUR WAIST CAN TAKE THE ATTENTION, THIS BELT BUCKLE WILL GRAB IT!

ROADSIDE REGALIA: TAIL LIGHT Belt Buckle

REFLECTIVE MATERIALS MAKE DAZZLING ACCESSORIES.

HUNTING GROUNDS

This plastic cover from a car's tail light was found, literally, at the **side of the road** (the dedicated junk jewelry designer is never too proud to PICK UP TRASH!), but your local auto repair shop or the accessories department of a large store will have many different shapes of reflective plastic in stock.

design ideas

① The tail light cover makes a good belt buckle because of its hollow shape, which allows for the fabric part of the belt to fit inside. Let the piece of junk you have dictate what it is best used for. ② Glue on an up eye or two to any small piece of reflective material and add an earwire to create earrings that catch light and shimmer in darkness.

THE DEDICATED
JUNK JEWELRY DESIGNER IS NEVER TOO PROUD TO PICK UP TRASH!

Raw Materials

For the belt part, you can use anything that is flexible enough to be attached to the buckle; for example, a **strip of suede** or BRAID of heavy ribbon.

HOW TO

All that was needed to transform the taillight cover into a belt buckle was a plastic rod secured to the middle of the back. The rod is a piece of plastic that was once the arm of a cheap pair of sunglasses. We chose plastic because it was easy to cut to the right length with a pair of wire cutters.

HOW TO

Also, if you are gluing things together, you'll get a stronger bond if you join the same sort of material (plastic to plastic, wood to wood) and use the appropriate glue. In this case, a glue made specifically to join plastics provided a firmer join than an all-purpose glue would have. Again, you can ask your local hardware store for advice on the best adhesives to use on your junk jewelry.

Attach a rod to create a buckle.

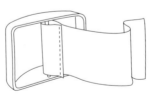

Sew or glue one end of the belt to the buckle.

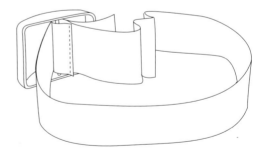

Wear the belt by pushing the other end of the belt through the buckle.

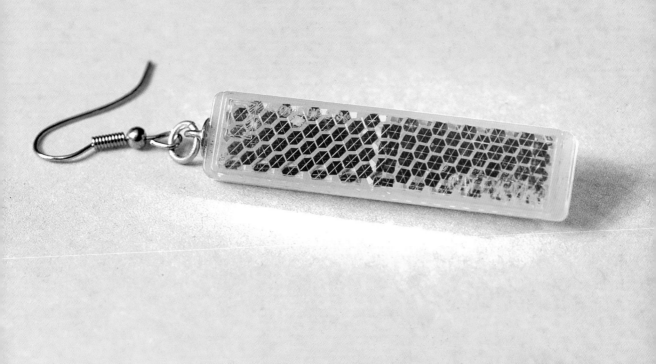

ANY STORE THAT CARRIES AUTOMOTIVE ACCESSORIES SHOULD HAVE "CAT'S EYE" REFLECTIVE PLASTIC IN DIFFERENT SHAPES AND COLORS.

THESE PLASTIC SHAPES CAME FROM THE SUPERMARKET AND HAD MAGNETS ON THE BACK.

HOBBY STORE LETTER earrings

HUNTING GROUNDS

HOBBY STORES have all sorts of miniatures, including wooden letter shapes. Try stores that sell educational kindergarten toys, too, as a source for wooden blocks and small toys. Lightweight **FOAM LETTERS** designed to be used for scrapbooking work, as well.

HOBBY SHOPS AND WEBSITES THAT SELL MINIATURE OBJECTS FOR DOLLHOUSES ARE GREAT RESOURCES FOR QUIRKY LITTLE OBJECTS

Raw Materials

Gather **SMALL LETTERS** whenever you see them. Even if they don't make a text message earring, they'll probably work as a pin or part of a necklace. And remember, when you're assessing the earring-worthiness of an object, that it must be **lightweight**.

design idea

Yes, you could wear your initials on either side of your head, but they won't mean much to passersby. What about an "O" and a "K" or *NO* or *SO* or *HA* or a pair of question marks instead? Or "Q" and "A" (to stand for Question and Answer) or "Q" and "T" (cutie)?

HOW TO

Either drill a hole through the letters or attach an up ring with glue. Add earring wires. Epoxy glue is probably the best choice here because you are joining two different substances. Epoxy is the adhesive that consists of two different parts that need to be mixed together. It dries quickly, so mix only the amount you need, and be sure to have everything ready before you begin. Set the letters upright by securing them in a homemade clamp such as a foldback clip or a heavy pair of pliers, as shown in the Game Piece section (page 78).

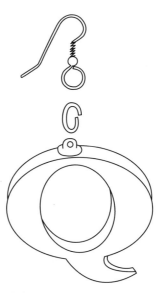

Assembling an earring.

WOODEN LETTERS FROM A HOBBY STORE.

Multicultural PENDANT

CELEBRATE THE BEAUTY OF THE UNUSUAL.

HUNTING GROUNDS

Visit shops selling goods from other lands and other cultures different from your own. You'll find beautiful and unusual things there, and once you start thinking about these objects as prospective pieces of jewelry, you'll see a whole new world of possibility. Visit your city's ETHNIC ENCLAVES. Shops selling Buddhist craft supplies have all sorts of interesting paper products with lovely **calligraphy**, and OLD COINS and beads. They also stock paper items made to look like luxury goods, which can be turned into wonderfully surreal junk jewelry.

When you travel even farther afield, you'll find lots more stuff. In Japan, seek out shops that sell facsimile food made out of plastic—the kind that restaurants often use to display their menu offerings. REALISTIC-LOOKING SHRIMP make funky earrings!

Raw Materials

Wear **anything unusual** on a cord. (But remember that heavy pendants can become dangerous, out-of-control missiles when you bend over!) Use PAPER ITEMS such as foreign newspapers and wrapping papers to make unusual pins.

design ideas

① Look for wrapped sweets from other countries; ② unusual stationery items and small kitchen utensils made of bamboo or wood; ③ foreign newspapers and packaging; and ④ religious items. ⑤ Soak funky labels off jars, or snip them from packaging. ⑥ Anything Asian looks great when worn with clothes that have a mandarin collar or "frog" closings.

WEAR
ANYTHING
UNUSUAL
ON A CORD.

HOW TO | ?

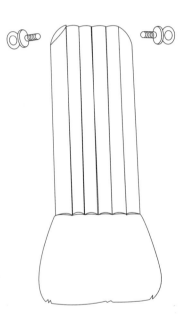

Eye screws transform a brush into a pendant.

A satin "frog" closure becomes an earring when an ear wire is attached.

String a leather thread through two coins, as shown.

① THE PAPER FACSIMILE OF A WRISTWATCH CAME FROM A BUDDHIST SUPPLY OUTLET. AT THESE STORES, YOU CAN BUY SURREALISTIC ITEMS MADE FROM PAPER THAT SYMBOLIZE VARIOUS WORLDLY GOODS. WE LIKED THE SYMBOLISM OF WEARING THIS WATCH, ATTACHED WITH SCOTCH TAPE, UNTIL IT WORE OUT. ② ASIAN-TYPE HABERDASHERY MORPHS INTO UNUSUAL EARRINGS. ③ TRADITIONAL BAMBOO BRUSHES USED FOR CALLIGRAPHY MAKE FOR A STRIKING PENDANT.

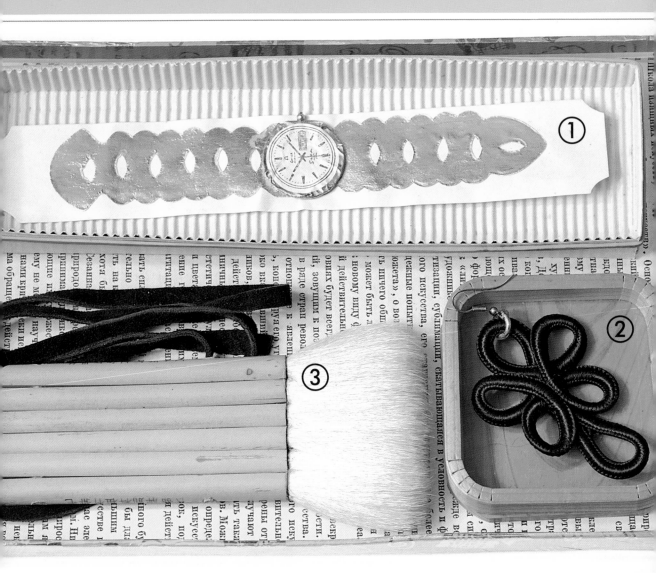

KEYBOARD COUTURE

SIGNS OF THE TIMES: ENTER, SHIFT, BACKSPACE.

HUNTING GROUNDS

About 2.5 million tons of electronics equipment are either THROWN OUT or recycled each year, so it shouldn't be difficult to find an old, unwanted computer keyboard. Try **recycling centers** or thrift shops.

KEYS CAN BECOME **CUFFLINKS, EARRINGS,** OR PART OF A NECKLACE

HOW TO ?

Attach a clip-on earring finding to a letter key.

Raw Materials

You'll probably need a **Philips head screwdriver** to open the keyboard. Start at the back and unscrew all the screws you can see. Lift off each layer until just the keys remain, dangling downward from the upside-down keyboard. Take a PAIR OF PLIERS and squeeze the sides of the empty plastic square that holds them in place. As you release them, they will fall out of the keyboard.

design ideas

① An empty square plastic stalk protrudes from the back of each key. You can drill a hole in it, or glue some sort of ring to it, depending on what you want to do with the key. ② Keys can become cufflinks, earrings, or part of a necklace. The earrings shown here were made by snipping off as much of the plastic stalk as possible, then gluing a clip-on earring finding to the back of the computer key.

HOW TO | ?

The longer keys have wire sections that can be used for attaching jump rings. The wire snaps into place, so it can be easily removed, bent upward, and then replaced. Check out the diagram to see how to do this.

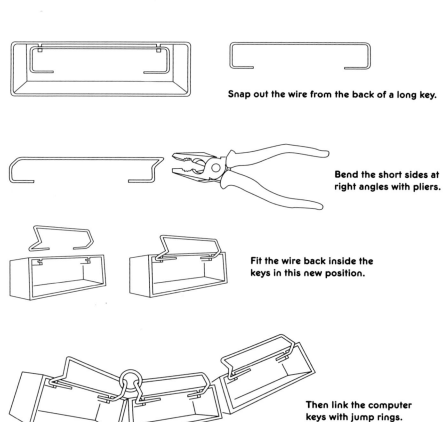

Snap out the wire from the back of a long key.

Bend the short sides at right angles with pliers.

Fit the wire back inside the keys in this new position.

Then link the computer keys with jump rings.

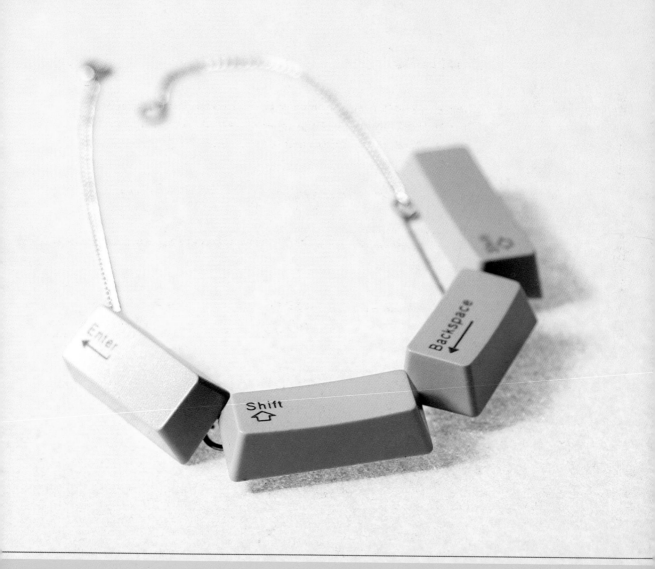

THE RECTANGULAR KEYS USUALLY COME WITH WIRE RODS, MAKING THEM IDEAL FOR JOINING TOGETHER.

DICE AND BEADS STRUNG ON ELASTIC THREAD.

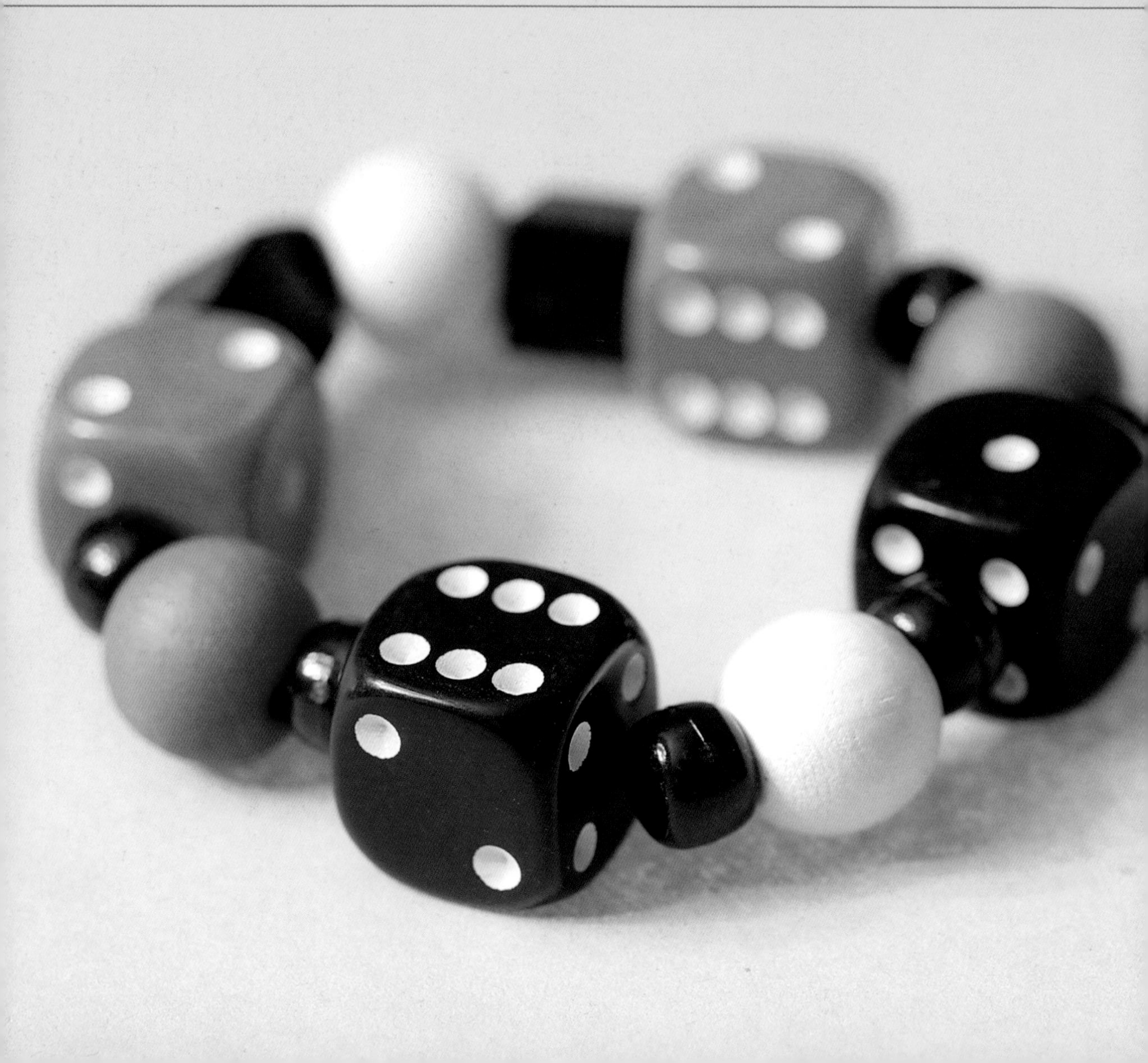

GAME piece glamour

HUNTING GROUNDS

Thrift shops are a good place to find old board games, and it doesn't matter if some of the pieces are missing. Look for Scrabble letters, dominos, **LEGO BLOCKS,** checkers (also known as draughts), *mahjong tiles,* and chess pieces, the older the better. Wooden and ivory pieces have a texture and ambiance that plastic lacks. **Wooden jigsaw pieces** have a more pleasing heft than cardboard.

DICE
ARE AVAILABLE FROM STORES THAT SELL BOARD GAMES, AND THEY COME IN MANY COLORS AND SIZES AND TYPES.

Raw Materials

A small drill is very useful for making holes. The holes can go through the length of the game pieces so you can use them as beads for bracelets. Or screw in TINY SCREW EYES so they can dangle from a neckpiece.

design ideas

① If you only have a few pieces, make a bracelet. ② If you only have one, make a pin, or use it as the centerpiece of a beaded necklace. Or go looking for more of the same kind of thing—they don't have to match. ③ The fake paper money from board games makes an interesting "jewel" when laminated.

HOW TO | ?

Drilling didn't work with the type of wood these black checker piece discs were made from, so we glued up rings to each side. To do this with a minimum of messiness, glue just one ring at a time, and, before you even open the glue, find a secure place to put the tiny item while the glue dries. A pair of heavy pliers can work well.

To make the spacers, take about one and half inches (3.8 cm) of silver wire and curl each end with round-nosed pliers.

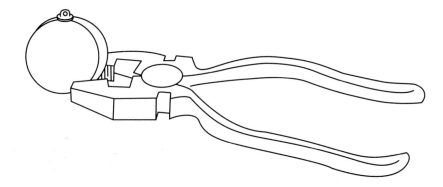

CHECKER PIECE NECKLACE

WOODEN CHECKER PIECES—JUST THE BLACK PIECES.

THIS PIECE FEATURES AN OLD IVORY AND EBONY DOMINO TILE. A HOLE WAS DRILLED THROUGH THE EBONY PART AND A LENGTH OF WIRE WAS INSERTED SO THE TILE COULD BE ATTACHED TO THE NECK RING.

LAMINATED STICKERS FROM A STATIONERY STORE WITH PINS GLUED TO THE BACK MAKE A QUIRKY STATEMENT.

Label PINS

HUNTING GROUNDS

Ask at the POST OFFICE or *stationery store* for labels that say things like Handle with Care. Or clip bits you like from comic books and **magazines**, or use FRUIT CAN LABELS, bar codes, foreign food labels, or *foreign paper money*.

Pieces of ANTIQUE PRINTED MATTER, such as tickets, labels, and brochures, are called ephemera. Older relatives may have some in scrapbooks that they are willing to part with. Or simply find old magazines and newspapers at TAG SALES and clip out weird, *dated advertisements* and photos.

Raw Materials

COMPANIES THAT LAMINATE ID cards and menus can coat any paper item you have to make it rigid. Or look in stationery stores for **self-sealing plastic envelopes** designed to protect and secure ID cards and luggage tags. Just glue a BROOCH PIN BACK on the flip side to make it into a brooch. A very easy way to get this look is to simply cut the paper you want to use to fit in one of those clear **plastic identity pins** that many companies use as nametags at gatherings. (You can cut these to be more square in shape, too, to make them look less like nametags.)

CLIP OUT WEIRD, DATED ADVERTISEMENTS AND PHOTOS.

design idea

It's not just paper products—many other flat items can easily become pins. Add a pin backing to felt flowers, small tops of jars or tins, clock faces, or any small, lightweight object.

HOW TO | ?

If the paper item you want to use is the wrong shape or not very exciting, glue it to a larger piece of colored or patterned cardboard and then cut that to size.

Make sure you glue the pin at the top of the back of the object—if the pin back is in the middle, the item will tend to tip forward when worn on lightweight clothing.

Several pins worn together in a cluster look even more interesting than just one.

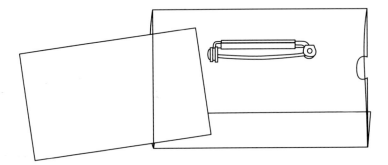

Slip any flat piece of ephemera into an identity badge.

OLD PACKAGE LABELS AND NEWSPAPER ADVERTISEMENTS USED TO MAKE PINS.

MINI SCOURING PADS BECOME FUNKY PINS FOR A LAPEL OR A HAT.

Flower SCOUR POWER

~YOUR CLOTHES CAN SAY "HOUSEWORK" AS WELL AS YOUR HANDS!

HUNTING GROUNDS

These scouring pads are smaller in size than usual. Your LOCAL SUPERMARKET may have them, or try a *hardware store.* For the leaves, we used a sheet of very fine-gauge brass from a hardware store, but you could use heavy tin foil, the kind you might find in a supermarket in the form of a single-use roasting or lasagna pan.

SOME OF THESE **FLOWERS** MIGHT LOOK CUTE ON METALLIC ACCESSORIES.

HOW TO ?

Raw Materials

The **foil or metal sheeting** can be cut with HEAVY-DUTY KITCHEN SCISSORS, but be very, very careful in handling the edges you make when you do this—they can be razor-sharp.

After you cut, smooth the edges with an old metal nail file (and consider wearing GARDENING GLOVES as you do so).

design idea

① Some of these flowers might look cute on metallic accessories such as silver- or gold-finish shoes, bags, or jackets.

To make the leaves, cut out the shape shown in the diagram on page 88. File down the edges, then place each leaf on a cutting mat. Take a blunt but pointed tool, such as a screwdriver or old knife or fork, and, pressing heavily, score the leaf first with a central line for the spine of the leaf. Then make lines radiating off the spine line. With a glue suitable for metals, attach the scouring pad to the leaf, then affix a brooch-back pin to the back of the leaf. To make a necklace just of leaves, you'll need to make a hole in each leaf. The kind of hole-punch used to make holes in sheets of paper for a three-ring binder works well. Join the leaves together by knotting them along a length of leather thong.

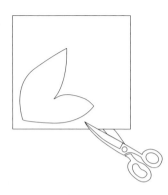
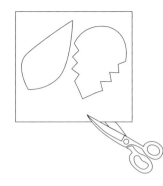

Cut leaf shape out of foil or copper sheeting.

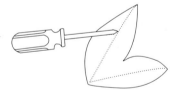

File the edges of the leaf shape.

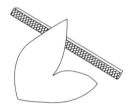
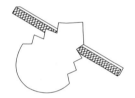
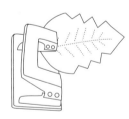

Use a hole punch to make holes in the leaves.

Knot the leaves onto a length of leather cord.

Score the shape with spine lines, then smaller lines radiating out of them.

TO MAKE A NECKLACE JUST OF LEAVES, JOIN THEM BY KNOTTING THEM ALONG A LENGTH OF LEATHER THONG.

THE ORDER OF THE FORK—MADE FROM A CHEAP, OLD PIECE OF CUTLERY—TO COMMEMORATE A SUPERB MEAL.

THE RIBBON Shop Medal

HUNTING GROUNDS

Odd buttons, clip-on earrings, or an old bar pin can be the starting point for a great medal, but the main component is a 3- or 4-inch (7.5–10cm) length of ribbon. If you don't have any at home, THRIFT SHOPS and stores that sell **sewing supplies** and notions sometimes have a table of remnants and odds and ends. Look at embroidered patches in the store, too, and curly embroidered "frogs"— knotted braid closures often seen on Asian-themed clothing.

Stores that supply uniforms may have pins spelling out a particular job, such as "conductor" or "controller", which can become a starting point. (An unexpected source if you are in Britain or one of the Commonwealth countries: *High school supply stores* often carry pins for prefects and head girls to wear to show their rank.)

ANYTHING THAT LOOKS VAGUELY LIKE MILITARY DECORATION... LOOKS AS GOOD AS A MEDAL.

Raw Materials

The most authentic ribbon for medals is STRIPED GROSGRAIN—the kind of ribbon with tiny ribs—but a **brocaded ribbon** works well, too. Sew a narrow strip of ribbon onto a thicker one to make a stripe, if you like. Add a COIN, an **orphaned earring**, or *washer* from the hardware store or any other small metal object.

design ideas

① To make a medal to honor an achievement or skill, find a charm or button to symbolize it: a bee for a spelling-bee winner, perhaps, or a tiny angel for someone who has been angelic. Then look for a piece of ribbon or braid that works well and put them together along with a brooch-back pin. ② If you're creating a medal as a gift, it's fun to make up a fake certificate to go with it, so you can designate the recipient as winner of "The Order of the Bee" or "The Angel Award" or some other imaginary honor.

HOW TO |

There are all sorts of ways to make a medal (see "a"–"e" on page 93), but here is a basic method that's easy to follow:

Fold a 4-inch (10cm) length of ribbon in half to find the midpoint.

With a pin, make two holes an eighth of an inch (3mm) apart in the middle of the ribbon at this halfway point. Secure a large jump ring through these holes.

Fold in the edges of the ribbon near the jump ring, as shown, and crease in place, making sure each side is even with the other. Fold in the raw edges at the top. Secure the crease and the raw edges with fabric glue, or use a needle and thread to sew in place.

Sew a brooch pin along the top, straight edge of the medal. This pin can extend at the sides, as shown in pin (a), or it can be just long enough to hide behind the ribbon. However, if the ribbon is very wide and the backing pin is short, you may need to glue or sew something inside the medal (such as a toothpick or a piece of cardboard) to stiffen it.

(a) (b) (c) (d) (e)

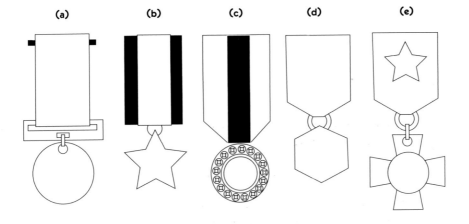

Use whatever you have to create a unique medal.

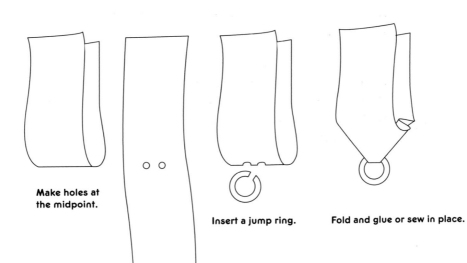

Make holes at
the midpoint.

Insert a jump ring.

Fold and glue or sew in place.

CREATE THE AWARDS YOUR FRIENDS DESERVE.

USE AN OLD FABRIC BELT TO ACCENT YOUR OUTFIT IN A NEW WAY

FAB Fabric BEADS

THE CHRISTO LOOK IN JEWELRY!

HUNTING GROUNDS

RANSACK YOUR WARDROBE for fabric belts that you no longer wear—the ones that are basically a long tube of fabric, without buckles. Look in *thrift stores* for these, too.

NO BELTS HANDY?
BUY A LONG, NARROW STRIP OF FABRIC AND MAKE YOUR OWN.

The size of the beads you'll need will depend on the width of the belt. For a wide belt, consider using lightweight foam balls from a craft supply store.

HOW TO

You'll need an uneven number of beads, either round or oblong, that are just the right size to slide inside the tube—not too small to get lost, not too large to strain the seams.

Raw Materials

The best belts to use are 1½–2 inches (3.8–5cm) wide and made of **THIN, PATTERNED MATERIAL** like silk, which knots easily.

design idea

No belts handy? Buy a long, narrow strip of fabric (at least a yard [.9m] long and make your own. If you take the homemade route, it's probably easiest to begin by looking for beads or foam balls in the size you want to wear. Wrap a measuring tape around the bead: half this measurement will be the width to make your fabric tube. Fold the fabric lengthwise, right sides together, and with a fabric marking pen draw a line at the width necessary. Sew along the length of the folded fabric, leaving the two short ends open, and turn right side out. After you have inserted the beads, knot them in place, and try on your creation. Then you can cut and sew up the ends to the best length.

If you've found a premade belt, fold it in half to find the halfway point. About an inch (2.5cm) to one side of this halfway point, slit the stitching to create an opening just large enough to slip in a bead. Insert all the beads, and push them along the length of the belt.

Find the halfway point again and position the middle bead there. Make a loose knot on each side of it. (At this stage, make the knots loose because you may have too many or too few beads in the tube and you might need to make adjustments.) Ideally, the place where you slit open the belt will be hidden inside one of these knots.

Slide the next bead up against one of the knots and make a knot. Do this until all the beads have knots next to them. Try on the necklace to check that there is enough fabric left at each end to make a bow, or at least a knot around your neck.

When you are happy with the way the belt looks, tighten the knots firmly up against the beads to secure them in place.

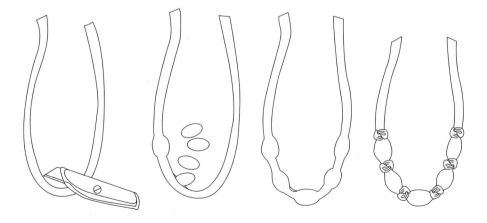

Make a small opening for the beads, slip them in, and knot in place.

THIS JEWELRY DOESN'T LAST LONG, BUT, THEN, NEITHER DOES VALENTINE'S DAY!

ARM CANDY (AND EAR CANDY, TOO!)

STAY AS SWEET AS YOU ARE.

HUNTING GROUNDS

Using real candy only makes sense if there is something very distinctive about it, such as an **imprinted slogan**; otherwise, you might just as well use beads. We've heard of gummy snakes and bears used as earrings, but really, this can get terribly messy! Best to **STICK WITH HARD CANDY** that has *distinctive markings*, like Valentine candy hearts. Even this won't stand up to much wear and tear, so consider it a one-day frippery.

STICK
WITH HARD CANDY THAT HAS DISTINCTIVE MARKINGS.

Raw Materials

Usually **HARD CANDY** doesn't go bad if it is kept dry. It's safest, however, to seal it, by painting it with **clear nail polish**. (Warning: Never give painted candy jewelry to young children or leave it lying around! Not only can this jewelry be a choking hazard, it can also be toxic.)

design ideas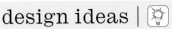

Necco Sweethearts Conversation Hearts® come in half-inch (13mm) and three-quarter-inch (2cm) sizes. ① Type into a search engine "old time candy shop," "old-fashioned candy," or "nostalgic candy" to find these and other unique possibilities on the Web. ② The wrappers and tins are decorative, too.

HOW TO |

Because nail polish dries so quickly, you can coat one side of the candy, wait fifteen minutes, then do the other. When they're dry, glue on up rings, and join with jump rings.

To go with the candy hearts, make a temporary bracelet from gold-toned elastic thread, cut to size. Join with the type of metal piece used to link keyring-type ball chain, clamped together with the ends of the elastic thread.

Cut a length of elastic thread to fit your wrist.

 Take the kind of fastener used with a ball chain.

Add the charm and push the ends into the fastener.

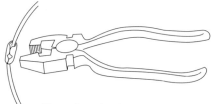

Clamp down hard with heavy pliers to crush the fastener together with the ends of the elastic thread.

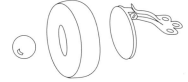

Constructing Life Saver ® earrings

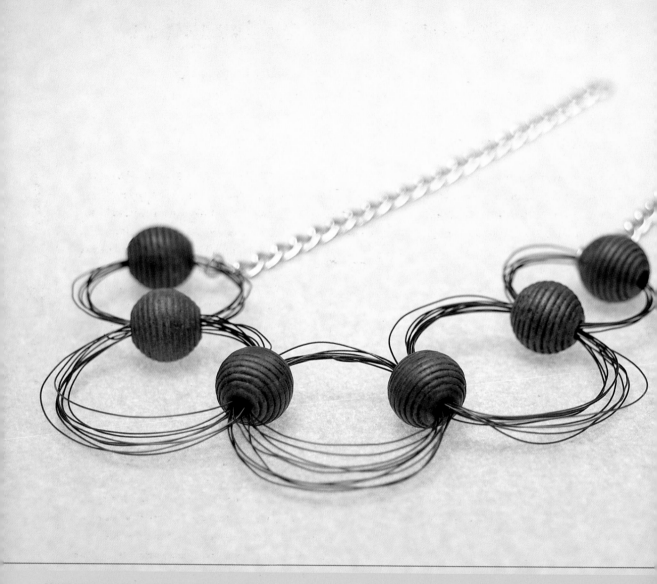

CRAFT WIRE COMES IN MANY DIFFERENT COLORS

HIGHLY STRUNG: Wire Necklace

THIS NECKLACE CAN BE MADE EITHER LARGE AND EXUBERANT OR SMALL AND DELICATE.

HUNTING GROUNDS

This necklace is easiest to make with the kind of wire that comes coiled into circles, such as picture wire. CRAFT SHOPS sell colored wire in this format. But any bendable wire is a candidate, and as mentioned earlier, some of the best wire for craft purposes comes from *telephone cable*. Next time you see an electrician working with wire, ask if he or she has any spare off-cuts available.

SOME OF THE BEST WIRE FOR CRAFT PURPOSES COMES FROM TELEPHONE CABLE.

Raw Materials

Most ELECTRIC CORDS consist of an outer coating, which houses several thinner plastic coated wires of different colors. (Of course, you must make sure all wires are unplugged and not connected to anything before you attempt to do anything with them!) To get to the inside wires, use a **craft knife** to pare away the outer plastic coating. Sometimes it will pull away once you've cut away some of it.

HOW TO

These necklaces were made from craft wire and picture hanging wire (the silver one). Each bundle is made up of wire about a yard (1m) long. For the joining beads, it's important to choose ones with large holes, so all the wire fits through. You need to thread the wire through two beads at a time.

design ideas

① Most people have a drawerful of computer cables that belong to long-gone hardware. Think before you toss those unwanted wires, those outdated, colored, curly telephone cords, or that old electrical wiring! These cables look great as cords for pendants or, as they are. ② Play with wire—it is easy to work with because it stays in place once it's shaped, and you can snip thin wire with heavy-duty scissors. ③ Look at "real" wire jewelry for inspiration.

HOW TO

Follow the diagrams. Start with the front central bundle, which will be the largest. Gradually decrease the size of the loops as you work toward the back of the neck. Adjust the position of the beads so that the necklace curves slightly.

You could hide the ends of the wire bundles inside the beads and glue in place if you want, but I like the look of messy circles and free-floating ends.

To finish the necklace, wind the wire around the end beads once or twice, and then fashion a loop on one side and a hook on the other.

Guide the wire through two beads, letting it maintain its tendency to coil

Take a new bundle of wire and another bead and repeat

When all the wire from one bundle is through, push the beads to opposite sides.

When all the wire from the bundle is through both beads, push one to the opposite side.

THE FLEXIBLE PLASTIC "MOTHERBOARD" USED FOR THESE EARRINGS CAME FROM INSIDE A COMPUTER KEYBOARD.

MOTHERBOARD Earrings

ELECTRONIC CIRCUITRY IS EASY TO WORK WITH.

HUNTING GROUNDS

Old electronic detritus can be seen on **GARBAGE NIGHT** in most big cities these days. Before you toss anything electronic, see if you can open it up and salvage any of the parts that look decorative. And if your own refuse isn't interesting enough, many cities have recycling centers: recycling outlets where industrial and commercial waste is donated so that it can be "repurposed." Additionally, some offices and public libraries have discarded circuitry receptacles where you can find *electronic doodads*.

> **COMPUTER** WIRING PRINTED ON FLEXIBLE PLASTIC SHEETING HAS A LOT OF POTENTIAL

Raw Materials

The **MOTHERBOARD** found in the main part of a computer is often brittle and difficult to work with unless you have an *electric saw*. It also tends to have scratchy lumps and spiky bits. The small piece of hard motherboard used for the piece on page 11 came from inside a cheap **alarm clock**—smaller objects often have more manageable components than computers.

But the kind of **COMPUTER WIRING** printed on flexible plastic sheeting has a lot of potential: It is easily cut with **SCISSORS**. Find it inside most **computer keyboards**.

design idea

Cut the flexible circuitry into strips or different shapes.

HOW TO | ?

Simply cut out whatever shape you want from a flexible plastic motherboard.
Cut thin strips or try other shapes, like these ovals folded in half.

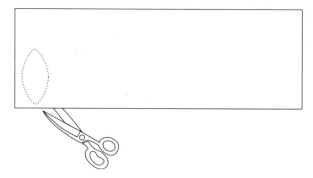

Cut an oval shape out of flexible motherboard, make a hole in each end, fold it in
half, and secure with a jump ring.

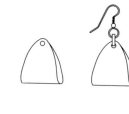

HANG AN EARRING WIRE FROM ONE CORNER OF A SQUARE OF MESH TO MAKE A CONE-SHAPED EARRING.

TILE MESH BAG Earrings

METALLIC MESH RESPONDS WELL TO LIGHT AND MOVEMENT, MAKING IT IDEAL FOR JEWELRY.

HUNTING GROUNDS

Scour THRIFT SHOPS for old mesh handbags, popular in the '50s and '60s and still made today. They come in colored enamel and **fabulous metallics**. You might also find these evenings bags in the back of your MOTHER'S OR GRANDMOTHER'S CLOSETS. They come in a variety of colors from gold, silver, and bronze to black, white, and red, and provide for endless possibilities in your jewelry designs.

Raw Materials

You will need a very SMALL PAIR OF PLIERS to work with the tiny **hooks** and **rings** that make up the mesh. There are two ways to start: You can use the pliers to undo one link at a time, or you can cut the mesh to the shape you want with WIRE CUTTERS. You can tidy up the edges later. Choose whichever method you find easier.

design idea

You can make rings and chokers from the mesh, too, but it seems to work particularly well as earrings, because the slightest movement makes the earrings shimmer.

HOW TO | ?

To make the oblongs, simply attach a length of mesh to the earring wires. This works well when the back of the mesh looks the same as the front. To make the cone-shaped earrings, start with an identical square of mesh for each ear. Attach a jump ring to one of the corners through two loops of mesh. Using two loops should help pinch the mesh back in on itself so it drapes nicely. If the back of the mesh isn't as attractive as the front, that's okay because it will be hidden inside the cone shape.

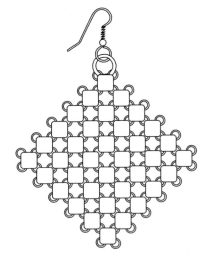

A square hung by one corner will drape into a cone shape.

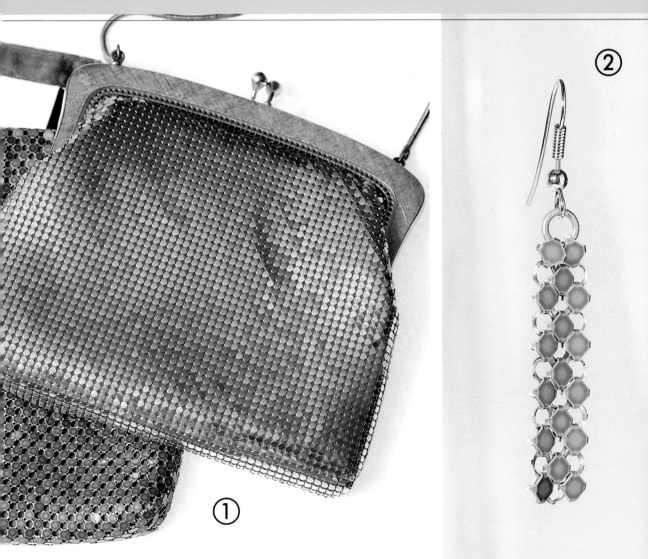

①

②

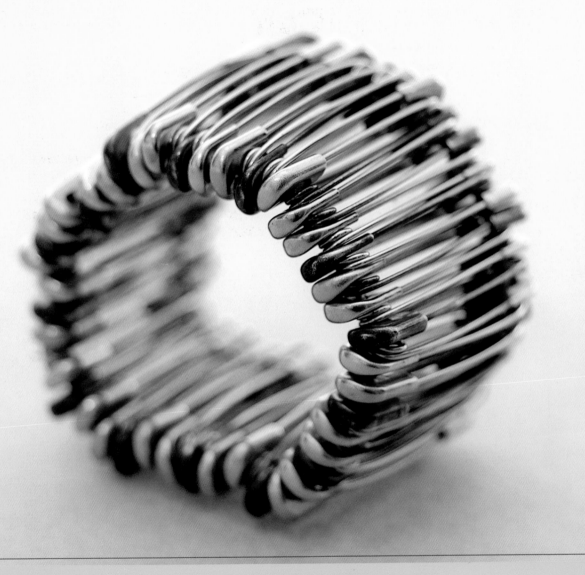

THIS CUFF WAS MADE FROM EIGHTY-ONE SAFETY PINS AND SOME METALLIC-TONED ELASTIC THREAD.

SAFETY PIN Cuff

AN ELEGANT EVENING BRACELET—OF SAFETY PINS.

HUNTING GROUNDS

LOOK FOR COLORED SAFETY PINS, TOO—THEY COME IN METALLIC COLORS LIKE PURPLE, GREEN, AND BLUE.

To reproduce this piece, the safety pins all need to be the same size, so the easiest way to acquire the raw materials is probably to BUY THEM IN BULK over the Internet, from a **sewing-supply** store. If the pins are too small, the elastic won't fit through them.

Raw Materials

For the piece shown here, 81 1½-inch (207cm) LONG PINS were used, in three different colored faux finishes: SILVER, GOLD, AND BRASS. You'll also need **fabric-covered elastic** with a metallic finish.

design idea

Look for colored safety pins, too—they come in metallic colors like purple, green, and blue. There are also painted safety pins available. Using all silver pins works well, too.

HOW TO | ?

To make the bracelet pictured, you'll need two lengths of elastic about 2 or 3 inches (5–7.5cm) longer than you'll need to go around your wrist. Tie one of these lengths in a big loose knot on one end. Start threading the pins in this order: the hinge end of a silver pin, the clasp end of a brass pin, the hinge end of a gold pin, the clasp end of a silver pin, the hinge end of a brass pin, the clasp end of a gold pin. Repeat this pattern until there are enough pins threaded to reach around your wrist. When they are all threaded, carefully undo the loose knots and secure the cuff into a circle by firmly knotting both ends of each piece of elastic together. Poke too-long ends back through the holes in the safety pins to hide them. Tie a loose knot. Thread the other length of elastic through the opposite ends of the pins. When they are all threaded, undo the loose knots, pull each elastic piece tightly, and knot firmly. Trim the ends, and poke the excess back through the holes in the safety pins to hide them.

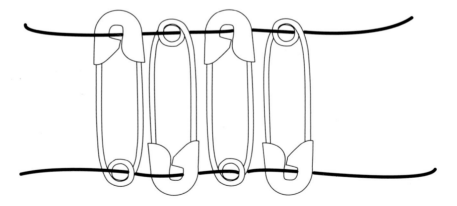

Thread safety pins alternating each end.

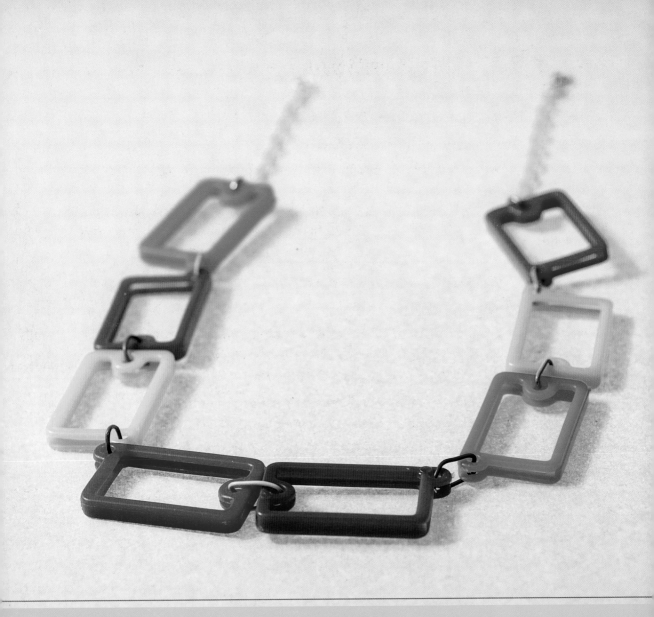

USE KEYTAGS AS "CHAIN," OR FILL THE SPACE WITH SOMETHING INTERESTING.

KEYTAG Creations

KEYTAGS MAKE CHEAP AND CHEERFUL CHAINS.

HUNTING GROUNDS

PLACES THAT COPY KEYS often sell interesting odds and ends, from key "blanks" to multicolored plastic doodads for sorting and labeling keys. Look in *hardware stores* and dime stores, too.

SMALL
PLASTIC OBJECTS IN BRIGHT PRIMARY COLORS ALL SEEM TO GO WELL TOGETHER.

Raw Materials

KEYTAGS become open squares when the paper and plastic inserts are removed. They also have handy holes for linking.

design ideas

① Small plastic objects in bright primary colors all seem to go well together. ② Empty keytags can become a "chain" when linked together. ③ Or use each tag as a mini-picture frame and insert a single letter or a message.

HOW TO | ?

The links used to join the keytags in the necklace are made from colored paper clips, cut into short lengths (about an inch [2.5cm] long), and bent into oval shapes with round-nosed pliers.

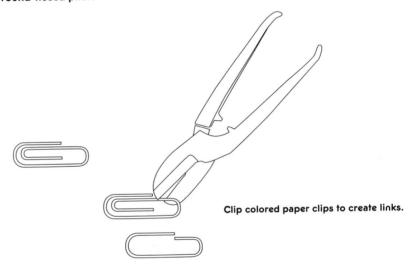

Clip colored paper clips to create links.

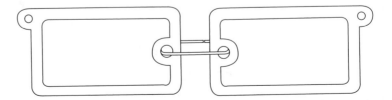

CHAMPAGNE CORKS COME WITH WIRE FASTENINGS, WHICH ARE USEFUL FOR JOINING THE TOPS INTO A NECKLACE.

CHAMPAGNE Top NECKLACE

CHEERS! WEAR THE MEMORIES.

HUNTING GROUNDS

Quick! Start saving **REAL WINE CORKS** before the wine makers of the world convert completely to plastic. (You may scoff, but once upon a time cotton thread

COZY

UP TO YOUR LOCAL RESTAURANTEUR AND ASK FOR HIS OR HER DISCARDS.

was packaged on cute wooden spools that could be recycled into many cool things, such as large beads.) If you save the tops from champagne bottles that celebrated good times, it will make this necklace all the more meaningful. Or just cozy up to your *local restaurateur* and ask for his or her discards.

Raw Materials

On close examination, you'll see that **CHAMPAGNE CORKS** have three parts: the cork itself, a metal medallion or disc on top that identifies the bubbly's vintage, and a "cage" of twisted wire. These all come apart—sometimes easily, sometimes not.

design ideas

① The metal medallion part of the top can be used by itself for a pin, or you could drill holes in several of them to thread for an unusual necklace. But the method we've used keeps some of the wire "cage" that's an inherent part of a champagne cork. ② Use just a few tops and a length of chain to make the necklace, or, as shown here, use enough tops to go right around the neck. You could use ribbon or cord for closing.

HOW TO | ?

Carefully lift the circular metal disc and the wire cage away from the champagne cork—you may need a tool like a pointed knife to do this. (No, not from the kitchen drawer! Keep an old one just for crafts.) With wire cutters, cut off the lower wire circle, leaving you with four corner ties. Don't worry if the metal discs get separated from the twisted wire. Using small pliers, twist back two of the twisted wires behind the metal disc. The other two need to be curled into circles so that jump rings can join them to the other tops. Join the tops with jump rings, as shown. If the metal discs won't stay put, use a little metal glue to keep them in place. Hook two lengths of chain to either side. Finally, attach a simple clip to one end as a closure.

Cut here →

Remove the cork and clip off
the bottom ring of the wire.

Twist the top two ties
to make rings.

Twist the bottom two ties
behind the metal disks.

Join the top ties
with jump rings.

A SHELL CAN BE EVEN MORE PRECIOUS THAN A DIAMOND IF IT'S A SOUVENIR FROM A GREAT VACATION.

HERE Today, GONE Tomorrow

THE ONLY "JEWELRY" YOU NEED ON VACATION.

HUNTING GROUNDS

Next time you GO FOR A WALK, look for objects you can turn into adornments. Feathers, shells, seed pods, flowers, a length of colored string, anything goes—it's all about *living in the moment*. You can find beauty and funkiness in the most ordinary things. Get creative and think outside the box—that feather or sea shell could make a wonderful, wearable souvenir.

> IT'S ALL ABOUT **LIVING** IN THE MOMENT.

Raw Materials

Tuck a FLOWER behind your ear, toss a curly length of **twine** around your neck—that's it! This "jewelry" won't last, but then, it's not meant to. In fact, that's the lesson: The only thing we can count on is that everything will change.

design ideas

① This is a laid-back approach to vacation dressing, and one that is fashionable, too. Items actually seen on the runways as necklaces include pieces of leather, rope, shells, and bootlaces. Madonna even started a trend with her "red string" bracelets associated with centuries-old Kabbalah, or Jewish mysticism. ② Take a cue from those silicon wristbands ("awareness bracelets") that look remarkably like wide rubber bands—you could make your own by actually wearing a wide rubber band with your own words inscribed on it!

HOW TO | ?

To take this look a bit further, attach a feather to an earring wire with glue or even Scotch tape. Anything with a hole in it can be slipped onto a wire neck circle. Or make a pendant: Thread a shell onto a strip of leather or ribbon, clear fishing line, electrical wire, or embroidery thread. If you have several items, add texture by tying a knot between each "bead."

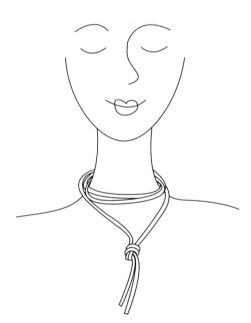

Seen on some of the most fashionable necks: a piece of string as a necklace

A speck of glue will hold the feather to an earwire.

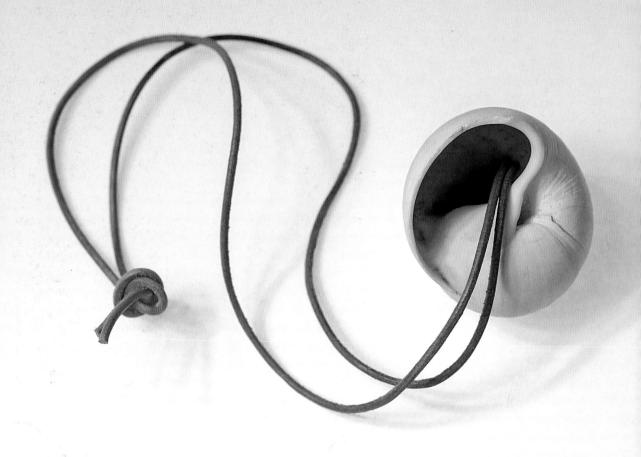

PART | ④

Never fear being vulgar, just boring.
—DIANA VREELAND

WEARING

WEARING JUNK JEWELRY IS AN ART IN ITSELF.

One should either **BE A WORK OF** *art,* or wear one.
—OSCAR WILDE

HOW TO WEAR junk jewelry

Why did mankind start wearing jewelry, anyway? Not just to display wealth. People were covering themselves with unusual decorations long before they were digging gold and diamonds out of the earth. Ancient people wore animal skins for warmth, but they also hung sharks' teeth and tiger claws around their necks for reasons of prestige, symbolism, and magical thinking. Clothing just keeps you warm, but jewelry from the remains of a fierce animal not only boasts that you killed the beast—you become, by association, brave and ferocious yourself! When the way of life in New Guinea was disrupted by Western civilization, it is said that some indigenous people adopted new symbols, such as a ballpoint pen worn through the nose, to reflect the changing culture.

Today, we wear expensive jewelry to brag, costume jewelry to decorate ourselves, and junk jewelry, perhaps, to demonstrate our individuality.

To carry it off, it helps if you revel in your uniqueness. Iconoclasts, especially those whose looks do not reflect conventional standards of beauty, usually put a lot of thought and effort into developing a personal sense of style, and thus create their own, distinctive kind of beauty. Elsa Schiaparelli (of whom Kennedy Fraser wrote in a 2003 issue of *Vogue* magazine, "She believed herself to be plain, if not ugly") is quoted as saying: "It is the woman who, not having the gift of great looks . . . has worked to make herself attractive, who is outstanding for chic."

Diana Vreeland (1903–1983), the influential editor of *Vogue* in the 1960s and consultant to the Costume Institute of the Metropolitan Museum of Art in New York, is a great example of this. Her distinctive clothes and accessories would probably not have worked so successfully if they had been worn by someone with less striking features.

Poise counts for a lot when you wear eccentric accessories. The harsh reality is that some of us were born with the God-given ability to feel comfortable in plastic sushi earrings and blowfly necklaces, and some of us weren't. There are women with so much *savoir faire* that they can wear gifts from preschoolers (acorns coated with gold, painted macaroni, lumps of papier-mâché covered in glitter) and look magnificent. Attitude and sense of style make the crucial difference between whether a piece of "jewelry" will look adorably whimsical or will be better enjoyed in the privacy of our own home.

For some, junk jewelry is a way to scream: "Hey everybody—look at me!" without doing any damage to the vocal cords. (It can help wearers to perfect a demeanor of studied nonchalance, even though, via peripheral vision, they may be keenly attuned to the subtlest reaction from every casual passerby.) When Punks first started to wear aggressively placed metal studs, dog collars, and safety pins as earrings in the late '70s and early '80s, they were hoping to arouse this kind of attention. Their jewelry was meant to look painful—and it was, usually eliciting a satisfyingly shocked reaction from those dressed more conservatively.

However, there is a fine line between looking magnificently outrageous and looking silly. The mere intention to wear something strikingly original does not, in and of itself, guarantee sartorial success.

The sad fact is this: You can love the idea of wearing junk jewelry but feel weird when you actually have it on. Take the case of one woman who was addicted to making and wearing junk jewelry. For every dress, she had the perfect accessories, for every holiday she wore the appropriate adornments. She made a vacation-themed necklace with miniature rubber flip-flops, palm trees, and shells to wear with a Hawaiian shirt. She chanced upon a lighting shop in the Little Italy neighborhood of Manhattan that sold chandelier parts and chose two faceted drops to make into her own, authentic, chandelier earrings for a special evening. She painted Valentine's candy with clear nail polish and attached jump rings to create a matching necklace and bracelet set. She created a choker from miniature colored pencils.

However, when she wore these things, people made disappointingly insensitive comments like, "Doesn't that stick into you?" and "Isn't that heavy?" Disillusioned, she gave them all to her friend, Ned. When Ned wore these things, she got oohs and aahs of delight and comments like, "Wow!" and "Fantastic!" and "Where can I get something like that?"

It's no reflection on your inner worth if you decide simply to admire junk jewelry from afar. But if you are determined to be a junk jewelry wearer, the following suggestions may help.

For some, junk jewelry is a way to scream: "Hey everybody—look at me!" without doing any damage to the vocal cords.

APPAREL principles

Apparel Principle #1: SYMBOLISM

Everything we wear sends a message about ourselves, especially jewelry. What are the subliminal messages contained in what you are wearing right now? It is very easy to inadvertently say something you don't mean. The label with a drawing of an elephant that you are wearing as a pin because you like the graphic may, to someone else, signify your political allegiance.

Alison Lurie, in her book *The Language of Clothes*, points out that a crucifix, for example, can mean many things. It can be worn decoratively, it can be a kind of good luck charm, it can serve as a warning to others, it can be an expression of religious faith, or it can be a protective talisman—or it can be all of these things at the same time.

Whenever you wear something quirky, it will inevitably draw attention to itself, and lead your audience to ponder its significance.

Apparel Principle #2: FOCAL POINT

It can be very chic to wear just one item of junk jewelry on the "canvas" of an all-black outfit. This makes the piece a focal point—that is, it leads the attention of your audience to where you choose, and diverts it from lingering on the parts of your body you'd rather people didn't dwell on.

You can also create focal points in an outfit with color, proportion, or strategic positioning. The eye immediately goes to something different in a sea of sameness (or to anything that moves, or to a place where two contrasting colors meet).

> *Talent is the choices we make*
> —STELLA ADLER

A chorus line of hearts becomes significant when worn along the sleeve for those who are familiar with the expression "wearing her heart on her sleeve."

Moreover, making just one piece of junk jewelry a focal point raises its credibility quotient. Your quirky Spam-label pin may be very amusing alone, but could look like a terrible mistake if you wear it with a whole lot of other, unremarkable costume jewelry.

That which is creative must first create itself.
—**JOHN KEATS**

Apparel Principle #3: SUITABILITY

One of the strange things about junk jewelry is how its message changes, depending on where you wear it. You'll notice this weird phenomenon when you wear a particular piece to different venues: The plastic shrimp earrings that drew so many admiring comments at your book club meeting turn into a big embarrassment among all the meticulously attired guests at your best friend's wedding. It is important to plan your ensemble with due regard for the occasion and the surroundings.

Be aware of the social references being invoked by what you wear, and decode the fashion statement you are making. Homemade jewelry might signal "I'm one of you," at one gathering and "I'm not taking this seriously" at another.

On the other hand, you may want to take advantage of junk jewelry's ability to make a social comment. In 1935, Schiaparelli made a statement about the devaluation of the franc by using gold sovereigns and French Louis coins as buttons.

You'd be surprised how much it costs to look this cheap.
—**DOLLY PARTON**

Less is often more, especially when it comes to directing attention to where you want it to go.

Chandelier earrings are unsuitable when doing yoga, for reasons relating to both aesthetics and personal safety.

Apparel Principle #4: ASSOCIATION

It is possible to become so entranced by a particular piece of apparel that you overlook the overall image you're presenting to the world. For example, a large hat on a small woman may make conjure up the image of a mushroom. And wearing a long metal zipper, wound around the neck, may be witty, but not if the total effect reminds people of Frankenstein.

When you are wearing jewelry in the form of objects, there is always the distinct possibility that you may bring to mind something unfortunate.

In general, people with strong features and large frames are more likely to look striking with large, bold accessories; petite people should wear more subtle, smaller items. If in doubt, get feedback before you hit the streets.

And if you are still in doubt, take it off.

Apparel Principle #5: ATTITUDE

Whenever you wear junk jewelry, wear it *con brio*. To wear it well, you have to be in the mood and feeling good about yourself. If you are embarrassed about it, others will pick up on your embarrassment. As with so many things in life, success is all in your attitude.

When you're feeling vulnerable and bruised, that may not be the best time to wear something you are unsure about. Wait until another time to bring out your earrings made of wisdom teeth or that bullet-casing pendant.

Then again, wearing something silly might cheer you up. Sometimes you want to be outrageous and crazy. When your attitude *du jour* is right and the stars are in alignment, you can wear anything

> *Reality is something you rise above.*
> —LIZA MINNELLI

and look fantastic. Life is short, so go for it. If your audience doesn't get it, so what? They simply have a different sense of humor.

And remember, the good thing about jewelry is that it's easy to slip off discreetly if you feel you've worn the wrong thing.

It is much more important to be yourself than anything else.
—VIRGINIA WOOLF

Apparel Principle #6: DEGREE

Junk jewelry can be very subtle or it can be in your face. When you choose what to wear, consider whether you prefer a more gradual dawning of recognition in the mind of your beholder: "Wait a minute, that isn't gold wire, those are safety pins!" Or a dropped jaw: "Oh my gosh, that woman looks as if she has a fried egg on her shoulder!"

When you don something that might raise eyebrows, complement it with clothes that are quirky enough to demonstrate that this is part of your sartorial philosophy, not some awful mistake. (In the case of a fried egg pin, for example, you might wear it on a yellow dress with chicken earrings.)

The more outrageous the item, the more skill it takes to wear it well. Subtle pieces can be worn more or less like "normal" jewelry, but craziness usually needs to be thought through well in advance, to avoid crossing that fine line between "Fantastic!" and "What was she thinking?"

Apparel Principle #7: THEME

Designers work with themes every season. Schiaparelli often based her collections on themes like harlequin clowns, pagan symbols, the military, the zodiac, and the circus, and she would commission jewelry and buttons to add to the effect. She also complemented the theme of her collection with buttons of diminishing sizes, or in the

If you feel at all doubtful about something you have on, go home and change.

There is subtle junk jewelry, and then there are items like a fried egg pin . . .

Junk jewelry can
turn a striped top
into a sailor suit.

Junk jewelry
lends itself to
subtle humor.
Accessorize your
serious business
look with a men's
tie and a bracelet
of paper-clip
chains.

shape of Christmas trees, peanuts, bullets, cupids, or bumblebees.

A theme can be as simple as wearing a button bracelet with a dress that features unusual buttons, or as elaborate as collecting all sorts of authentic nautical accessories to wear with your sailor outfit.

However, subtlety is the key to a look you will feel comfortable wearing—unless it is Halloween or you are going to a fancy dress party.

Apparel Principle #8: EDIT

To wear junk jewelry well, you have to be willing to integrate it into your total look. This involves a commitment that is no hardship for creative dressers: It calls for always carefully editing every ensemble and creating whole outfits rather than just throwing on something quirky.

For example, wearing a necklace of green frogs is wonderful, but wearing head-to-toe green—lime dress, pistachio tights, olive shoes—will set off that green frog necklace to its best advantage.

In fact, you may find yourself making junk jewelry specifically to go with particular ensembles.

> *There are flowers everywhere for those who want to see them"*
> **—HENRI MATISSE**

In anything at all, perfection is finally attained not when there is no longer anything to add but when there is no longer anything to take away.
—ANTOINE DE SAINT-EXUPÉRY

---

resources

ONE PERSON'S JUNK IS ANOTHER PERSON'S
JUNK JEWELRY!

Raw materials that I find exciting you may consider ho-hum. You will probably develop your own sources, but here are some suggestions as a starting point.

JEWELRY FINDINGS

- jewelrysupply.com
- firemountaingems.com

JUNK

There are two ways of finding junk: one can look for a particular item, or let chance guide you to fabulous finds. The Internet is a great resource for finding just about anything using a keyword search. Sites I've come across include:

- safetypins.com
- makingfriends.com

To stumble across something you didn't know you were looking for, it's easier and more fun to browse at quirky shops in person, although, as in real life, the more you explore on the Internet, the more likely serendipity will occur. For example,

I came across the craft site articusstudiodesign.com (which has interesting products like poetry word beads) when I was looking for something completely different.

MY FAVORITE SOURCES
for Unexpected Treasures

THRIFT STORES such as the Salvation Army and yard and garage sales. These are great for finding old costume jewelry that can be taken apart and remade; children's toys (look for quirky items like Barbie doll limbs); buttons; old board games; low-quality, bendable cutlery; old keyboards and small, broken electrical appliances, to take apart for the interesting bits inside.

To see if there is a thrift store near you, check out thethriftshopper.com for a national directory.

CRAFT STORES. As well as buying findings here, look for items designed for other crafts that can be used for "jewels." For example, miniatures made to furnish dollhouses and the tiny people created for use in making architectural models make great junk jewelry.

STATIONERY OR HARDWARE STORES. Look for unusual paper clips, cardboard tags, labels, miniature pencils, and rubber bands in stationery stores. Look for small nuts, bolts, washers, wire, and chain at hardware outlets.

DOLLAR STORES. You might find beads to add to your jewelry and cheap plastic items including luggage tags, small toys, and key rings.

NATURAL HISTORY MUSEUM GIFT STORES. Great for rubber animals and insects, semi-precious stone beads, and sea shells.

INSPIRATION

I find it truly awe-inspiring to see what people have made from junk! The great thing about the Internet is the way you can find others who share a passion, no matter how obscure it may be. The indie crafts scene is booming on the Web. Check out the following craft magazines and websites—none of them traditional or boring. And I'll be putting up examples of pieces I've made on my website, eldershaw.com. Come visit!

Some great online crafting magazines:

CRAFT MAGAZINE at craftzine.com
For "a non-commercial DIY zine which provides easy, inexpensive yet damn cool projects," Visit thriftdeluxe.com

MAKE MAGAZINE at makezine.com

READYMADE MAGAZINE at readymademag.com

Some great craft forums:

- supernaturale.com
- churchofcraft.org
- graftster.org
- getcrafty.com
- threadbanger.com
- craftyvixens.tribe.net

Interesting online shops:

- tattydevine.com
- fredflare.com
- lianakabel.com

Books on fashion psychology:

- *The Language of Clothes* by Alison Lurie
- *Open and Clothed* by Andrea Siegel

SELL YOUR JUNK JEWELRY

Create your own online store and find like-minded crafters in the message boards at esty.com and mintd.com

There are indie crafts fairs all around the country. One of the biggest is the Renegade Craft Fair: find it online at renegadecraft.com.

index